Royalty UNVEILED

Royalty UNVEILED

IRIS DUPREE-WILKES

But you are a chosen generation, a royal priesthood, a holy
nation, His own special people, that you may proclaim
the praises of Him who called you out of darkness
into the marvelous light 1 Peter 2:9 (NKJV).

authorHOUSE®

AuthorHouse™ LLC
1663 Liberty Drive
Bloomington, IN 47403
www.authorhouse.com
Phone: 1-800-839-8640

Published by AuthorHouse   07/02/2014

ISBN: 978-1-4969-2037-9 (sc)
ISBN: 978-1-4969-2038-6 (e)

Unless otherwise indicated, Scripture is taken from the New King James Version Copyright 1979, 1980, 1982 by Thomas Nelson, Inc.

Scripture marked NIV is taken from the HOLY BIBLE, NEW INTERNATIONAL VERSION, Copyright 1973, 1978, 1984 International Bible Society. Used by permission of Zondervan Publishing House. All rights reserved.

Scripture marked AMP is taken from Internet Web site: www.biblegateway.com, AMPLIFIED, Copyright 1995-2010, The Zondervan Corporation.

Scripture marked NLT is taken from Internet Web site: www.biblegateway.com, NEW LIVING TRANSLATION, Copyright 1995-2010, The Zondervan Corporation.

Scripture marked GWT is taken from Internet Web site: www.biblegateway.com, GOD'S WORD TRANSLATION, Copyright 1995-2010, The Zondervan Corporation.

Scripture marked KJV is taken from Internet Web site: www.biblegateway.com, KING JAMES VERSION, Copyright 1995-2010, The Zondervan Corporation.

All definitions taken from:
Webster II New Riverside University Dictionary, Copyright 1984, 1988; by Houghton Mifflin Company

1 Peter 2:9 (NKJV) But you are a chosen generation, a royal priesthood, a holy nation, His own special people, that you may proclaim the praises of Him who called you out of darkness into the marvelous light.

Contents

Acknowledgements

To my Husband and Children:
Michael Wilkes, my husband of 19 years, and to my beautiful children; Omar and Alexis thank you so much for all of your love, support, and understanding. I pray that each of you will fulfill the call that God has on your life. I love you!

To family:
Connie (deceased) and Olivia Dupree the best parents in the world, thank you for all of your love and support you have given throughout the years. I thank God for our family unity. I love you!

To my Editing Committee
We did it once again ladies, thank you so much for seeing this project to completion. I thank God for your commitment and dedication. I love you, and I am grateful for all that you have done. Together we have accomplished much, thank you!

Most of all I would like to thank God for making all of this possible, and for the many readers that shall read this book and grow thereof. I am grateful for life, health, and a strong mind; thank you God for empowering me to be who you created me to be. I am grateful for each one of you as you allow the spirit of God to speak to your heart throughout this book. May you receive all that God has for you and your household in Jesus name, Amen.

Customers Reviews

From the Book: The Making of a Beautiful Vessel

Ms. Lisa Ebron
Greenville, NC
Your book, "The Making of a Beautiful Vessel" has inspired, motivated and encouraged me to continue to "yield completely to God." As I continue to yield, I will evolve into that "Beautiful Vessel" God has designed me to be!! Thank you for allowing God to use you to be a blessing to me and so many others!!

Mrs. Darlene Wilkes
Clarksville, TN
"The Making of a Beautiful Vessel" is an easy tool for anyone who truly desires to get closer with God and to gain understanding of what God has for them. As you obey the Word of God as outlined within the various chapters it leads you on the pathway to freedom. ***The word is a lamp for my feet, a light for my pathway- Psalm 119:105.*** By understanding God's Word it puts you on the direct path where God wants you to be.

Mrs. Gwyda Myers
Greenville, NC
"The Making of a Beautiful Vessel," **Chapter 11, 'Trouble and the Open Door, the Battle in Between'** spoke to me while I was in a transitional period. My options were to either move forward or stay stuck. It helped me to move out of low living and pushed me forward. I could not continue to stand and look but instead I had to go through the open door. It helped me to forget about what I was in as I came to terms with God's plan for my life, a future with an expected end.

Mrs. Vassie Barrett
Greenville, NC
"The Making of a Beautiful Vessel" made me come out of denial. It gave me a face to face moment with myself. Allowed me to be real with what was in my heart. I could no longer cover or try to hide my issues; it brought me to a place of surrender. I was then free enough to go to God and receive my healing.

Mrs. Arnetha Gaddy
Greenville, NC
"The Making of a Beautiful Vessel" develops the mind to come out of a place of bondage to a place of surrender. It causes you to rely on the purposes and plans of God instead of the purposes of man. My area that I've turn to when it seems hard and times got rough was Chapter 5 *'Trust God for More.'* The book informs us that we should allow God's Spirit and nature to operate freely in our lives. As a believer one can allow the cares of life to cause them to be bound, simply for not trusting in God. Trusting God changes you and your circumstances. "The Making of a Beautiful Vessel" gives you examples of life stories to assist you, ensuring that you are not alone and you can make it. This book captures the mind, body and soul to be loosed and set free so you can walk in the destiny of the Kingdom of God.

Ms. Kimmy Phillips
Raleigh, NC
Thank you, thank you, thank you for being obedient to the voice of God! "The Making of a Beautiful Vessel" is most definitely a blueprint from our Father!

The beginning journey of reading "The Making of a Beautiful Vessel" was so challenging for me! I have to admit I picked it up and put it down quite a few times before completing it. The reflection of personal experiences was staring back at me from the written words of truth in the choices made throughout life! I couldn't hear the voice of God for the broken path of personal experiences. As I began to read the provided scriptures and take notes and speak the written prayers out loud the anointing of the provision began to manifest more and more! Becoming one with our Creator is very challenging! **Chapter 10**, *'Experiencing Your Gethsemane'* has been my daily path changer to why I am a "Beautiful Vessel" as I continue my Christian journey through to the end!

Again, I thank you for being obedient to the voice of God! Love you very much!

Introduction

Understanding Who You Are – "Royalty"

Lord as you pour the oil of royalty upon my head
I shall not be fearful or intimidated
to rule and reign in my position as kings
and priests in Jesus' name. Amen.

God desires for you to know who you are. He wants you to understand that you are indeed royalty. He has given you power and authority to command His word to come alive, and to manifest itself in your life. You my brother and sister are royalty for you are in the royal lineage of Jesus Christ. Since you are connected to Jesus Christ, you shall also reign with him. Regardless of your circumstances "royalty" has a measure of faith to move beyond what it looks like. The royalty of God can overcome all circumstances, it will not be held in bondage or in a state of poverty. ***Revelations 5:10 (NKJV) And have made us kings and priests to our God; and we shall reign on the earth.***

As a king and priest are you reigning on earth? What is going on in your midst? Have you allowed your life to be down trodden with low living, succumbing to the tyrants of men? This is not the life that God has called you to; He desires to give you more than what you are currently facing. However, you must step out in faith and believe God for your outcome, for there is indeed more to you than what people see!

Repeat after me:
I am a king and a priest, and I shall reign on earth now! I will not be easily tricked, swayed or deceived by the devil. I will operate in the authority that God has given me, and I will live my life like the king and priest that I am.

Understanding the power and authority of Kings
A king has authority over those in whom they rule. Just as a man and a woman are different, with various gifts and abilities so it is with kings

as well. No two kings are exactly alike but yet all have royal status. Even in the life of King Solomon, the Lord exalted him greatly and gave him royal majesty unlike any other king before him. Solomon prospered and the people obeyed and submitted themselves to him. God had a plan for Solomon's life, and it went beyond being anointed as king (*1 Chronicles 29:23-25*).

Prior to Solomon being anointed as king, his father David helped to prepare him for what was to come. *1 Chronicles 22:6-13 (NKJV) 6 Then he called for his son Solomon, and charged him to build a house for the LORD God of Israel. 7 And David said to Solomon: "My son, as for me, it was in my mind to build a house to the name of the LORD my God; 8 but the word of the LORD came to me, saying, 'You have shed much blood and have made great wars; you shall not build a house for My name, because you have shed much blood on the earth in My sight. 9 Behold, a son shall be born to you, who shall be a man of rest; and I will give him rest from all his enemies all around. His name shall be Solomon, for I will give peace and quietness to Israel in his days. 10 He shall build a house for My name, and he shall be My son, and I will be his Father; and I will establish the throne of his kingdom over Israel forever.' 11 Now, my son, may the LORD be with you; and may you prosper, and build the house of the LORD your God, as He has said to you. 12 Only may the LORD give you wisdom and understanding, and give you charge concerning Israel, that you may keep the law of the LORD your God. 13 Then you will prosper, if you take care to fulfill the statutes and judgments with which the LORD charged Moses concerning Israel. Be strong and of good courage; do not fear nor be dismayed.*

David spoke life and blessings to his son, asking the Lord to give him wisdom and understanding so he could fulfill the plans of God for his life. Solomon was about to walk into his royal position. It was in David's mind to build the temple, but not in God's plan. Therefore, David had to be obedient to follow God's plan for the future generations. The Lord told David that Solomon would be a man of rest from all his enemies. His reign would be free from constant warfare.

Fathers should be making preparations for their children's futures. They must understand their royal status and speak the Word faithfully over their seeds. Men of God what has the Lord spoken to you about your child/children? Whose plans will you prepare for the future generations, yours or Gods? I encourage you to speak life over your son(s) and daughter(s).

(Insert your child/children name) may the Lord be with you and may you prosper and build your house for the Lord (the kingdom in you). May the Lord give you wisdom and understanding so that you will obey the word of the Lord all the time. May you walk as the king and priest that God has called you to be. May you prosper and be in good health all the days of your life. May you fulfill your purpose in God and His kingdom. May you always know and understand your identity in Christ and walk in His ways. May you submit yourself to the Word of the Lord in all things. *(Insert your child/children name)* be strong and of good courage, do not fear nor be dismayed. Walk in your royal authority! May you open your mouth and speak like the king and priest that God called you to be, in Jesus' name. Amen.

After David encouraged his son he told him what had been prepared so he could complete his assignment. Not only did King David speak in his son's life, but he also made preparation for his son to complete what was given unto him. How are you making preparations for your son(s) and daughter(s) to complete what God has spoken?

> *1 Chronicles 22:14-16 (NKJV)* [14] *Indeed I have taken much trouble to prepare for the house of the LORD one hundred thousand talents of gold and one million talents of silver, and bronze and iron beyond measure, for it is so abundant. I have prepared timber and stone also, and you may add to them.* [15] *Moreover there are workmen with you in abundance: woodsmen and stonecutters, and all types of skillful men for every kind of work.* [16] *Of gold and silver and bronze and iron there is no limit. Arise and begin working, and the LORD be with you."*

King David had prepared the talents of gold, silver, bronze and iron beyond measure in abundance. He also provided workers in abundance for the tasks that his son was to complete. The only thing that Solomon had to do was to arise, get up, and begin working! The Lord was with him. The Lord equips and prepares before hand all those in whom He calls. As children of God, you must seek to prepare beyond measure, in abundance for the next generation.

As I speak about David's royal authority, I pray you are able to get a clear understanding of the power and authority you have as kings and priests of God. If King David, a man of flesh, was able to make preparations for his son in such great measures, imagine the resources and supplies the father has prepared for you. Are you in proper position so you can receive the resources and supplies? He has unlimited supplies and resources with your name on them without any limitations. Walk in your royal authority and receive them.

> *1 Chronicles 22: 17-19 (NKJV) ¹⁷ David also commanded all the leaders of Israel to help Solomon his son, saying, ¹⁸ "Is not the LORD your God with you? And has He not given you rest on every side? For He has given the inhabitants of the land into my hand, and the land is subdued before the LORD and before His people. ¹⁹ Now set your heart and your soul to seek the LORD your God. Therefore arise and build the sanctuary of the LORD God, to bring the ark of the covenant of the LORD and the holy articles of God into the house that is to be built for the name of the LORD."*

David spoke to all the leaders of Israel to help Solomon. He used his royal authority and commanded them to help. He reminded them of several facts as to why they should help, after all God had done for them. He tells them, "This is your set time to seek the Lord!" Arise, get up and build the sanctuary, no excuses needed or allowed. As leaders and members of the body of Christ are you doing your part in the plans of the Lord for the kingdom? What are you doing? If not, I speak to your spirit to arise! Get up! Has not the Lord been good to you, why sit ye here? Get up and do the work of the Lord. Walk in your royal authority and complete what God has given you to do. Arise and stop making excuses, do your part, get up!

As Solomon began to walk in his royal position as king the Lord appeared to him and asked what shall I give you (1 Kings 3:5)? As you begin to walk in your royal position what shall the Lord give you? As you understand your royalty what do you desire of the Lord? Keep in mind He has already called you a king and a priest. With that being said and with proper understanding of your kingly rights, what do you need? As you seek to answer the question, remember as a king certain things are already yours.

Prayer: Lord we seek the kingdom of God's success in everything that you have purposed and planned for us to accomplish and to complete on this earth. We release your will to be established forever in our lives over all affairs now and forever in Jesus' name. Amen.

The power and authority of Priests

A priest in the Old Testament was an official minister or worship leader in the nation of Israel who represented the people before God and conducted various rituals to atone for their sins. Priests acted as mediators between people and God offering sacrifices so that sin might be forgiven.

Each sacrifice was a demonstration that the penalty of sin is death (Ezekiel. 18:4, 20) and that there can be no forgiveness of sin without the shedding of blood (Hebrews 9:22).

The office of the priest was fulfilled in Jesus Christ. The son of God became a man (Hebrews 2:9-17) so that He might offer Himself as a sacrifice once to bear the sins of many (Hebrews 9:28). Hence, there is no longer a need for priests to offer sacrifice to atone for man's sin. A permanent sacrifice has been made by Jesus Christ through His death on the cross. Now He calls you and I kings and priests because we as priest have direct access to God through Christ. As we begin to share the message of Christ with others, we then begin to execute the function of a priest.

God has given you access to all things, nothing can be withheld or denied because you are his priests who shall reign on earth.

Revelation 1:6 (NKJV) ... and has made us kings and priests to His God and Father, to Him be glory and dominion forever and ever. Amen.

When God looks at you He sees a king or a priest; He doesn't see someone unqualified, insignificant or unworthy. In His plan, you are not the tail, but the head. Kingdom resources are at your disposal if you will only believe and take hold of them. You don't have to just get by, you have an inheritance and a future filled with success in Christ. You are called to reign on earth. Walk in it!

- Let the oil of royalty continually fall upon your head in Jesus' name.
- Let the oil of royalty descend upon your family throughout the generations in Jesus' name.
- Let the oil of royalty come upon your business bringing increase and insurmountable measures beyond limits in Jesus' name.
- Let the oil of royalty begin to locate you and your seed to escort you to your royal position in Christ, opening doors and gates of breakthrough as you and your seed continually rule and reign in Jesus' name. Amen.

Chapter 1

THE POWER AND AUTHORITY
OF ROYALTY

Power: is the ability or strength to perform an activity or deed.
Authority: is the moral right or privilege.

Jesus Christ has power and authority and has bestowed it upon His followers. You can have power to perform a task but not the authority to do it. The power and authority of royalty can look at a situation and say, "It doesn't matter what it looks like." Royalty refuses to be in captivity, held on lockdown, or stuck to what looks or seems impossible to the natural eye.

Luke 4: 31-36 (NKJV) 31 Then He went down to Capernaum, a city of Galilee, and was teaching them on the Sabbaths. 32 And they were astonished at His teaching, for His word was with authority. 33 Now in the synagogue there was a man who had a spirit of an unclean demon. And he cried out with a loud voice, 34 saying, "Let us alone! What have we to do with You, Jesus of Nazareth? Did You come to destroy us? I know who You are—the Holy One of God!" 35 But Jesus rebuked him, saying, "Be quiet, and come out of him!" And when the demon had thrown him in their midst, it came out of him and did not hurt him. 36 Then they were all amazed and spoke among themselves, saying, "What a word this is! For with authority and power He commands the unclean spirits and they come out."

Jesus looked at the situation and said, "It doesn't matter;" and began using His power and authority to cast out the unclean demon. Jesus did not allow what He saw with His natural eyes to determine the outcome of the situation. He did not allow what He heard to deter Him from using what was in Him. The unclean demons began to speak, but Jesus refused to entertain what was being said. Instead, He rebuked the unclean demon, and He called evil into submission by using his power and authority.

It didn't matter how things looked, Jesus did not lose control over the voice of the demon; He refused to entertain the devil. You must learn to look at what you are going through in the natural and say, "It doesn't matter," and mean it from your heart. It's easy to say it doesn't matter when you are not faced with a terrible situation or an urgent need. However, what about when you have a disaster on your hand that is causing great damage, pain, and suffering in your life. How will you handle it? Will you be able to say it doesn't mater or will you gather it in your heart, taking matters in your own hands and become bitter within? It's at this point in your situation that you must say it doesn't matter from your heart, knowing full well that Jesus will work it out as you speak to that spirit that troubles you. Don't allow it to hold you in captivity, or on lock down. You need to rebuke the voices of the enemy and call evil into submission, use your power and authority. Tell them to be quiet because it doesn't matter.

As you begin to use the royal power and authority over life situations, your outcome will be different. *For with authority and power He commanded the unclean spirits and they came out.* This man's life was changed, and it left those who witnessed the commands of the voice of the Lord in amazement. *Then they were all amazed and spoke among themselves, saying, "What a word this is!"*

> *Luke 4:36 (NKJV) For with authority and power He commands the unclean Spirit and they came out.*

Jesus was able to speak with power and authority because He used His voice to speak what He was given from God the Father and evil spirits obeyed. *John 8:28 (NKJV) … as my father taught Me, I speak these things. John 12:49-50 (NKJV)* *⁴⁹ For I have not spoken on My own authority; but the Father who sent Me gave Me a command, what I should say and what I should speak. ⁵⁰ And I know that His command is everlasting life. Therefore, whatever I speak, just as the Father has told Me, so I speak."*

God gave Jesus Christ a voice that Jesus has in turn given His followers (you & I) a voice that has power and authority to speak and change things.

> *Luke 10:19 (NKJV) Behold, I give <u>you</u> the authority to trample on serpents and scorpions, and over all the power of the enemy, and nothing shall by any means hurt you.*

We have the authority to trample on our enemy who sometimes comes in the form of a serpent; He is wicked and rebellious because of his destructive influence. He is our hostile foe, hateful, cunning, sly, and malicious. He has a poisonous stinger, and he has the ability to cause great harm.

Satan's power:
- Rules a vast kingdom of fallen angels and demonic beings *(based on Matthew 12:26-29, 25:41; Ephesians 6:12; Revelation 12:4, 7, 9).*
- Is the prince of the power of the air and has the whole world in his power *(Ephesians 2:2) (1 John 5:19b).*
- Is the god, ruler, and deceiver of the whole world *(2 Corinthians 4:4) (John 12:31, 14:30).*
- Has every person who is not "in Christ" (a believer) as "his child" and under his power and always opposes *(Matthew 13:24-30, 36-42, esp. verse 38; Ephesians 2:2-3).*

Despite the definition, traits and power of Satan you have been given the authority to trample over all the power of the enemy. To trample is to beat down with the feet, bruise, crush or destroy, or tread heavily.

Given this kind of authority you shall win over the enemy. Let us not remain in a state of defeat, however, it's time to deal with the enemy.

It's time to put a halt to his destructive and evil plans. So the next time that old sly, evil serpent and those poisonous mouth scorpions, and your hostile enemy and foe shows up in an attempt to destroy you, put him in his place. Refuse to allow the enemy power over you. Use your voice and command him to be quiet. Resist the devil, and he will flee. With the power and force behind you, trample the devil, and he will be under your feet, **not even allowed to speak**. As you do, it shall bruise, crush, and destroy the devil with his evil, malicious, and wicked ways. Give God praise as you trample upon your enemy. As you trample on something you must be in a moving position, you can't stand still. A lot of you have been standing still with little to no movement when that old sly devil or malicious serpent, appeared before you with his wicked and evil intentions. You choose your outcome by what you do. Now is not the time to stand still, pick your feet up and tread heavily, bruise, crush, and destroy your enemy. You have been given power and authority over him.

Stop accepting what the enemy is speaking in your ear, it is poisonous, and he's trying to launch his greatest attack against your life. He desires to pierce you, causing great damage and harm. The devil is known as passive, he's sly, cunning, hateful, and hostile. He comes with the intent to kill, steal, and destroy. Nothing he tells you is for your good. His plans are evil against you, your home, your family, and your job. He roams around in many forms seeking someone to devour. *2 Corinthians 11:14-15 (NKJV) ¹⁴ Satan himself transforms himself into an angel of light. ¹⁵ Therefore it is no great thing if his ministers also transform themselves into ministers of righteousness, whose end will be according to their works.*

Even in all of this you have been given authority and power over the enemy. It does not matter how much force is behind him. God has given you royal power and authority and nothing shall by any means hurt you. If God said it, shall it not come to pass? Every word out of the mouth of God is true, and it shall not return empty. The word comes with power and authority to do what He said it would do.

God will contend with your enemies and foes:

- *Romans 16:20 (NKJV) And the God of peace will crush Satan under your feet shortly.*

- *Isaiah 59:19 (NKJV) When the enemy comes in like a flood, the Spirit of the LORD will lift up a standard against him.*

- *Psalm 27:1-3 (NKJV) [1] The LORD is my light and my salvation; whom shall I fear? The LORD is the strength of my life; of whom shall I be afraid? [2] When the wicked came against me to eat up my flesh, my enemies and foes, they stumbled and fell. [3] Though an army may encamp against me, my heart shall not fear; though war may rise against me, in this I will be confident.*

- *Psalm 28:7 (NKJV) The LORD is my strength and my shield; my heart trusted in Him, and <u>I am helped</u>; therefore my heart greatly rejoices, and with my song I will praise Him.*

- *Psalm 68:1-2 (NKVJ) [1] Let God arise, let His enemies be scattered; let those also who hate Him flee before Him. [2] As smoke is driven away, so drive them away; as wax melts before the fire, so let the wicked perish at the presence of God.*

- *Psalm 68:6 (NKJV) God sets the solitary in families; He brings out those who are bound into prosperity; but the rebellious dwell in a dry land.*

- *Psalm 68:21 (NKJV) But God will wound the head of His enemies, the hairy scalp of the one who still goes on in his trespasses.*

- *Psalm 144:1-2 (NKJV) [1] Blessed be the LORD my Rock, who trains my hands for war, and my fingers for battle— [2] My loving-kindness and my fortress, my high tower and my deliverer, My shield and the One in whom I take refuge, Who subdues my people under me.*

- *Psalm 44:5 (NKJV) Through You we will push down our enemies; through Your name we will trample those who rise up against us.*

- *Proverbs 16:7 (NKJV) When a man's ways please the LORD, He makes even his enemies to be at peace with him.*

- *Psalm 37:39 (NKJV) But the salvation of the righteous is from the LORD; He is their strength in the time of trouble.*

- *Psalm 56:11 (NKJV) In God I have put my trust; I will not be afraid. What can man do to me?*

- *Psalm 138:7 (NKJV) Though I walk in the midst of trouble, You will revive me; You will stretch out Your hand against the wrath of my enemies, and Your right hand will save me.*

- *2 Thessalonians 3:3 (NKJV) But the Lord is faithful, who will establish you and guard you from the evil one.*

Prayer: I pray that you walk in your royal power and authority from this day forward. You shall rule and reign in the earth realm. I call royalty, righteousness, and the riches of God into every aspect of your lives and that of your seeds for many generations, in Jesus' name. Amen.

REFLECT AND JOURNAL:

Chapter 2

THE ROYAL MINDSET

"How to keep control over your mind"

A royal mindset is that of Christ. ***Philippians 2:5 (NKJV) "Let this mind be in you which was also in Christ Jesus."*** Having the mind of Christ formed within you, is the ability to think like Christ. If you are struggling with an out of control mind, you must subdue it by exercising authority or influence over it. Nothing in your life can exceed your level of thinking. Your creativity, your dreams, and your vision for life deal with your mind and your thought process. ***2 Timothy 1:7 (NKJV) "God has given you a spirit of power, of love and of a sound mind."*** A sound mind is a disciplined and healthy mind.

- My mind is renewed by the Word of God; therefore, I forbid thoughts of failure and defeat to inhabit my mind.
- I refuse to be limited or hindered due to the thoughts in my mind. In the name of Jesus, I LOOSE spiritual knowledge, revelation, insight, understanding, wisdom, truth, discernment, diligent searching, freedom, and permanent deliverance in my life. The Lord causes my thoughts to become agreeable to His will and so my plans are established and will succeed.

If you do not control your mind, others will. Mind control is a weapon of Satan to snare the believer. He wants to distort your thinking by producing evil and ungodly thoughts within you. The devil will do all he can to corrupt your mind. ***2 Corinthians 11:3(NKJV) But I fear, lest somehow, as the serpent deceived Eve by his craftiness, so your minds may be corrupted from the simplicity that is in Christ.*** He comes to deceive the world, the devil knows if he can utter truth, he does so only that you will listen to him and eventually believe what he mixed with a lie. The devil is a liar; he is the father of lies. He wants to destroy, deceive, and divide you and your family with his lies.

You must recognize what you are thinking about and what voices you give ear to. When people try to live by the reasoning of their natural mind, they find themselves lusting or desiring things they consider normal. This is the bait of Satan. He will have you go over and over within your mind what to do by the nature of your flesh. This gives an opening to the devil to gain control over your mind. When this happens, you have chosen to dismiss the Word of God and allowed demonic forces to lead your thought process.

Remember in **Revelation 20:8(NKJV) "...Satan will go out to deceive the nations."** Satan's objective is to weave you into his web of lies and deception at any cost. Therefore you must know who you are:

- You are a king and a priest.
- You are royalty, you have a righteous mind!
- You will not be easily swayed or deceived.
- You will triumph in Christ! 2 Cor. 2:14
- You were created for good works! Eph. 2:10
- You are sufficient for every task! Phil. 4:13
- You shall overcome every obstacle! John 16:33
- Health and prosperity is yours, you are healed, whole and healthy! 3 John 2

Isaiah 26:3 (NKJV) You will keep him in perfect peace, whose mind is stayed on You, Because he trusts in You. When your mind is steadfast and stayed on Christ then it's firmly fixed in place. It will **not** be subject to change; it's **firm** in belief, determination, and (or) adherence. In order to be kept in perfect peace you must firmly fix your mind on Christ. He has the ability to be at rest in the midst of any storm or chaos. *Psalm 29:10-11 (NKJV) ¹⁰ The LORD sat enthroned at the flood, and the LORD sits as King forever. ¹¹ The LORD will give strength to His people; the LORD will bless His people with peace.* Even though there was a flood, He did not allow it to snatch His peace or to destroy the foundation of the earth. Instead, He operated in His sovereign power and authority. He was in control. In other words, He let it be. He sat enthroned at the flood. It was divinely sent to deluge against human wickedness *Genesis 6:5 (NKJV) Then the LORD saw that the wickedness of man was great in the earth, and that every intent of the thoughts of his heart was only evil continually.* He allowed the flood to occur to change what was happening at that particular time on earth. It was all for a divine purpose. However, in the midst of purpose being formed, He strengthened His people and blessed them with peace.

There may be a flood in your life right now, and it may appear in sickness, pain, brokenness, unhealthy relationships, toxic situations, sexual abuse, molestation or disease. How are you going to get God's attention in the midst of your situation? God is on His throne even in the midst of your situation. He allows the storm and chaos in your life for a divine purpose. But remember in the midst of your storm He will strengthen and bless you with peace. Call upon God to come and see about you, His ears are attentive to your cry.

- I'm hurt and confused – help Lord
- I'm fatigued, worried and stressed - help Lord
- I'm distracted - help Lord
- I have allowed bitterness to grow within my heart - help Lord
- I want revenge and to retaliate against my attackers – help Lord
- I feel defeated with this attack on my mind – help Lord

Our God is awesome, He is King over all! He will turn the bad into good, the ugly into beauty, the negative into positive, and the hurt into healed. *John 8:36 (NIV) So if the Son sets you free, you will be free indeed.* He has given you a sound and disciplined mind. You wear the attire of a conqueror! You have been designed to overpower the enemy. God's plan is to bless and not to curse, to make alive and not to kill, to prosper and not to cause you to fail. Remember I say to you, *Matthew 18:18 (NKJV) Whatever you bind on earth will be bound in heaven, and whatever you loose on earth will be loosed in heaven.* You cannot bind or loose anything if you are silent or if you allow the devil to control your tongue. You cannot fight the devil with a jacked up mind or a closed spirit. You must bind him from your thoughts; refuse him entry into your life. As a conqueror, you must maintain control at all times in your life.

Job 33:5 (NKJV) Set your words in order before me; take your stand. What do you need on today? Open your mouth and set your words in motion. ***Job 38:12-13 (NKJV)*** The Lord reveals His omnipotence to Job, He asks, [12] ***"Have you commanded the morning since your days began, and caused the dawn to know its place,*** [13] ***that it might take hold of the ends of the earth, and the wicked be shaken out of it?***

In other words like Job, you need to remember who God is. He commanded the morning to arise and for daybreak to come forth. He arranged for the wicked to be shaken out of your mind, your heart and your life. God has commanded for things to take place. Open your eyes and see what is standing before you. ***1 John 4:4 (NKJV) He that is within me is greater than he that is in the world. Romans 8:3 (NKJV) If God is for us who can be against us?*** He has already prepared great things for you on today so don't allow the devil to keep you silent or to keep you in a place of constant turmoil in your thinking. The Lord is enthroned and gives strength to his people and blesses them with peace. Therefore, with Christ's mindset operating within you -the royal mindset of a conqueror- you will have complete control over your mind.

Psalm 11:4 (NKJV) The LORD is in His holy temple, the LORD's throne is in heaven; His eyes behold, His eyelids test the sons of men. It may appear that He is not involved in what is happening in your life, His eyes are aware, know that He does see, and He will act. Therefore, you shall draw upon the spiritual resources that He has provided for you. **(Insert your name)** will attack the strongholds and plans of the enemy that has been put in place against her/him. I command in the name of Jesus Christ that the enemy release my mind, my will, my emotions, and my body completely. They have been yielded to the Lord, and I belong to Him. (You now have a righteous mind and a royal mindset.)

Psalm 10:16 (NKJV) The LORD is King forever and ever. He always wins. His ruling is final and He has victory over all. No one can oppose

His glorious rule. He has empowered you to keep moving forward. I have outlined three important steps to help you to have a royal mindset (that of Christ). Ask the Lord to help you to become the person you were created to be.

Step 1: Surrender

Psalm 37:7 (GWT) Surrender yourself to the LORD, and wait patiently for him.

You must give God permission to walk through your life daily, and expose anything and everything in you that is not of faith. ***Psalm 139:23-24 (NKJV) ²³ Search me, O God, and know my heart; try me, and know my anxieties; ²⁴ and see if there is any wicked way in me, and lead me in the way everlasting.*** Will you allow the light of God to search your heart to see what's operating within you? God wants to lead you into a better place, a place of peace and joy. Are you willing to surrender and allow God to have his way in your life?

God loves you, and he will not allow anything to happen in your life that has not been Father-filtered. Thus, no matter what you see or what you understand to be happening, trust God to work out His purpose in your life.

A surrendered life will trust God's purpose without understanding the circumstances. You will not use manipulation or try to force your agenda in an attempt to control the situation. You must learn to wait on God's timing without knowing how He will provide. His way and timing is the perfect fit for your situation.

Just as Jesus surrendered himself to God's plan, you must do likewise. ***Mark 14:36 (NLT) He prayed, "Father, everything is possible for you. Please take this cup of suffering away from me. Yet I want your will, not mine".***

This level of maturity in walking in full surrender to God's plan doesn't come easy. In Jesus' case, He agonized so much over God's plan, that He sweated drops of blood, but He still surrendered despite things going on in his mind. Surrendering is hard; it requires intense warfare against our self-centered nature. It requires you to give yourself to the Lord fully knowing He will work for you and not against you. He has your best interest at heart.

Prayer: Now that you are ready to fully surrender, pray this prayer daily. (Write this prayer on an index card and carry it with you.) **"Father, in the name of Jesus, I am now willing to place my body, my soul, my spirit, and my entire life into Your hands. I ask that You place me into Your perfect will for my life. From this moment on, I will choose to stay fully surrendered to You all the days of my life, and I will allow You to lead and direct my life in the direction that You want it to go in Jesus' name. Amen.**

As you surrender your life to God, from your heart, it will bring you into a realm with God that will completely change the course of your entire life. If you are willing to make this full surrender to the Lord, He will take full control of your life and steer it in the direction that He will have it to go.

Step 2: Putting off (negative habits) & Putting on God's thoughts

Ephesians 4:22-24(NIV) ²² You were taught, with regard to your former way of life, to put off your old self, which is being corrupted by its deceitful desires; ²³ to be made new in the attitude of your minds; ²⁴ and to put on the new self, created to be like God in true righteousness and holiness.

These verses exhort us to ... put off concerning the former conversation (behavior) the **old man** (old self), which is corrupt according to the deceitful desires; and to be new in the spirit of your mind; and then put on the **new man** (the new self), created to be like righteousness and true holiness.

A renewed mind, is one that has done two things: It has put off any sin, corrupt thinking, or any barrier that would quench God's Spirit, and it has put on the Mind of Christ (2 Corinthians 10:5). The process of renewal means to exchange one thing for another. In other words, when we put off and put on, we're exchanging our thinking for God's thinking. God wants us to have His Mind (His thoughts, His viewpoint) in every situation. He wants us to have the supernatural ability to discern everything that happens to us from His perspective. He does not want you to get bogged down and buried by your negative thoughts, feelings or by what's going on in your life. If you can see from His perspective, then you will be able to soar above your circumstances.

The renewal of the mind does not happen automatically, you must spend time with God in reading, studying, and meditating on the Word of God. God has called us to be royalty. Decide now to accept this role. He has chosen for you to walk in your heritage that He has provided for you. Remember: No matter how cleansed and consecrated you are on the outside, know you are being changed on the inside and deep in your heart. Are you thinking like royalty or as slaves, fearful and unworthy?

It is my desire that you be transformed through the renewing of your mind. No longer compromising with the ways of the world, or yielding to the enemy's attacks. As the Lord opens your eyes and reveals to you those areas in your life that are not pleasing him I pray that you remove the sin and weight. Allow Him to work in you to cleanse all ground that would give the devil a foothold in your life. I claim in every way the victory of the cross over all satanic forces in your life, in Jesus name. Amen.

Step 3: Now walk in the newness of your mindset.

A walk reveals there is motion; it demonstrates movement in some direction. Therefore, where you are right now is not your final destination. This newness of life defines the walk. It is resurrection life. His resurrected life now becomes our life. We do not merely exist in this Christian life, there is motion – we are moving in a direction. When we allow His life to define our life, we are in a moment by moment experience of being conformed to Him in our mind, will, and emotions. This life is completely different from our life before Christ, it really is a new life.

> *2 Corinthians 5:17 (NKJV) Therefore, if anyone is in Christ, he is a new creation; old things have passed away; behold, all things have become new.*

Walking in newness of life means:

- Reading God's Word every day: *"The entrance of thy words gives light: it gives understanding to the simple" Psalm 119:130 (NKJV).*

- Praying to God and praising Him at all times: *"Be anxious for nothing; but in everything by prayer and supplication with thanksgiving let your requests be made known unto God" Philippians 4:6 (NKJV).*

- Loving our brethren and sisters: *"Beloved, let us love one another, for love is of God; and everyone that loves is born of God, and knows God" 1 John 4:7 (NKJV).*

- Being considerate to other people, and helping them whenever we can: *"Therefore, whatever you want men to do to you, do also to them" Matthew 7:12 (NKJV).*

- Not taking part in the ungodly activities of the world: *"Wherefore come out from among them, and be ye separate, saith the Lord, and touch not the unclean thing; and I will receive you. And I will be a Father unto you, and ye shall be my sons and daughters, saith the Lord Almighty" 2 Corinthians 6:17, 18 (KJV).*

- Above all else, loving God with all our being: *"Thou shalt love the Lord thy God with all thine heart, and with all thy soul, and with all thy might" Deuteronomy 6:5 (NKJV).*

If you follow the three steps outlined for you, it will help you to operate with your royal mindset. Surrendering is an act of releasing self and allowing the Lord to rule. Putting off old and putting on new changes you from who you were to who He has called you to be. Operating in your new mindset (royal mindset) is to be 100% all of who Christ calls you to be. It's the ability to think higher like Christ.

I speak forth words of healing to you now: Your mind is renewed by the Spirit of God and where the Spirit of the Lord is there is liberty. Your mind is liberated and you are set free from the things in your past. You are happy, whole, and healed! You have been created in the image of God. The Spirit of Christ operating in you makes you different than you were before. You are a new creation and forever changed. All things are possible for you because you believe. Confess that your mind is healed, your thought process is restored, and your life is full of hope and expectation! You have a righteous mind and you will not allow the enemy to rule your thoughts. You have the mindset of Royalty and will not be easily distracted by the evil plans of the devil. You shall be all that God has called you to be.

REFLECT AND JOURNAL:

Chapter 3

DISPLAYING ROYAL LOVE – LOVE 10

1 John 3:16 (NIV) This is how we know what love is: Jesus Christ laid down his life for us. And we ought to lay down our lives for our brothers and sisters. Jesus is our example of love. Love is more than a feeling, it's more than emotions. *Romans 5:8 (NIV) But God demonstrates his own love for us in this: While we were still sinners, Christ died for us.* Love is an action word. Christ laid down His life for you and I, this is known as agape love. Christ's agape love rescues us from the punishment that we deserve. It's the kind of love that God has for us, and we are commanded to have for others. *John 13:34 (NIV) "A new command I give you: Love one another. As I have loved you, so you must love one another.* This is a love that is not earned, it's given freely. It's the ability to love the undeserving, despite disappointment and rejection. This is real authentic love without pretensions or expectations.

1 Corinthians 13:4-7 (NIV) ⁴ Love is patient, love is kind. It does not envy, it does not boast, it is not proud. ⁵ It does not dishonor others, it is not self-seeking, it is not easily angered, it keeps no record of wrongs. ⁶ Love does not delight in evil but rejoices with the truth. ⁷ It always protects, always trusts, always hopes, always perseveres. In this passage of scriptures God tells us what love is and what love is not.

Love …	Love…
• Is patient – slow to anger, forbears • Is kind - gentle • Rejoices with the truth – loves the truth • Protects – covers, endures patiently • Always trusts – in all things in God's Word • Always hopes – believes, looks forward to with desire • Always perseveres – bears up against Suffering	• Does not envy – is not jealous • Does not boast – does not brag • Is not proud – thinking highly • Is not rude – dishonor others • Is not self-seeking – **Philippians 2:4** • Is not easily angered – not easily provoked • Keeps no records of wrongs – does not track inventory of wrongs • Does not delight in evil – does not delight in what is contrary.

As you allow the love of God to flow freely from your heart, will you display royal love? Make sure you keep your love radar on at all times. In the midst of your furnace, how do you display love? You must learn to:

1. Love the **unfaithful**, those who have *hurt and abused* **you** leaving unwanted pain because of their selfish desires.
2. Love **those who have hidden agendas**, *schemes and lies* and seek to launch an attack against you in an attempt to clog the main artery in your heart.
3. Love **those who you look up to (mentor)** but due to their actions and decisions have caused *great discouragement* in your heart.
4. Love those who have **stolen years of your life** due to their *obsession and evil habits.*

5. Love those who **walked out on you** leaving you to *raise the children* and to figure out the next step for their future.
6. Love those who often **devise evil plans** *against your life* and that of *your children.*
7. Love those who **introduced you to** *toxic drugs, illicit sexual activity,* and *unhealthy relationships.*
8. Love those who may have **molested or raped** you, taking away what was *innocent and precious.*
9. Love those who have **killed or murdered** your *love ones.*
10. Love those who are in an **adulterous relationship** with *your spouse.*

Can you learn to love beyond conditions and barriers? How are you showing love in the midst of your furnace? God gave me ten situations to approach in this chapter to see if one or if all of these situations happened directly to you, would you still be able to display love? In this chapter we will refer to these ten situations as **"Love 10"**.

It's easy to love those who in turn love you. But what about those who say they love you and their actions do not display that love, will you still love them? How will you respond in the midst of your furnace while trying to live right? As a king and a priest unto God (Revelations 5:10) can you walk in your royal authority in the midst of your furnace? Allow God's agape love to be seen in your actions toward your brothers and sisters, despite how they treat you. Be patient, refuse to be easily angered, do not keep a record of the wrong things people do to you. Be kind and allow your love for them to protect and cover the situation.

Despite what the enemy attempted to do, the three Hebrew boys responded with love. They refused to give in to the devil. Love endures all things. They were able to persevere against suffering. As they stood for what was right, honest, and just, they ended up in the hot fiery furnace. They did not allow what they were going through to deter their love. They did not get angry, but instead they put their trust in God. He kept them safe in the midst of their affliction.

As you stand for what is right you too may end up in the furnace of affliction. If you do, know that God will keep you safe as well. There may be times in your life where a circumstance from **"Love 10"** may happen to you, will you stand in the midst of trouble and do what's right? How will you respond? God allows your enemies seasons in your life to attack. He leaves them in a certain location with power to test, prove, refine and to chastise you for your good. He wants to show you the state of your heart. For within the deepest part of your heart God sees, He's aware and wants you to be free. Despite your enemies' actions, can you reach out and still display love?

As I listed **"Love 10"** I thought about my life, if any of those things happened to me, how would I respond? I said, "Lord, help me, because you see the state of my heart." And I realized my direct response to **"Love 10"** would show me what's lurking within my heart. God allows us to go through seasons of pain, times when you have to deal with lies, schemes, backbiting, brokenness and your mind being captured by the enemy, to show you the truth from your heart. He allows the painful process and the bitter ordeal to help develop your Christ-like, kingly anointing. In other words, without **"Love 10"** in your life how can you know anything about struggle or how can you learn to progress or to grow? **"Love 10"** will help you to grow stronger in God as he sharpens your coping skills by developing your listening skills. He wants you to grow in understanding and receive patience in dealing with others while learning about true love and forgiveness. God's agape love has genuine concern for all people.

God wants your faith to increase, therefore; He has allowed undeserved enemies to test you. He wants you to know that He is greater within you and those undeserved enemies will serve as a teaching tool. Stop focusing on how life is not fair, the setback, the heartaches, the sickness or financial difficulties. These things are a part of living in an imperfect world broken or laden with sin. Don't allow what you go through in life to stop you from moving onward to full maturity. God allows your enemy to attack, only to make you better and stronger as part of your testimony. *Romans 5:3-4 (NKJV) ³We also glory in tribulations, knowing that tribulation produces perseverance; ⁴ and perseverance, character; and character hope.* Disappointments and tribulations can bring about perseverance. When things don't go right, persevere, stick it out to the end, and don't give up. As you persevere through hard times it helps to develop and strengthen your character. Your final result is that you should have hope in spite of your circumstances, and this hope is based upon trust in the love of God. Hope is not based upon things going right. Hope is based upon the fact that God loves you in spite of disappointments and tribulations.

"Love 10" does not determine God's measure of love for you. His love is unconditional; therefore, you must deal with these underserved devils. *Judges 3:1-4 (NKJV) ¹ Now these are the nations which the Lord left, that He might test Israel by them, that is, all who had not known any of the wars in Canaan ² (this was only so that the generations of the children of Israel might be taught to know war, at least those who had not formerly known it), ³ namely, five lords of the Philistines, all the Canaanites, the Sidonians, and the Hivites who dwelt in Mount Lebanon, from Mount Baal Hermon to the entrance of Hamath. ⁴ And they were left, that He might test Israel by them, to know whether they would obey the commandments of the Lord, which He had commanded their fathers by the hand of Moses.* Those in whom the Lord left in the land had a purpose. He did not leave their friends, but their enemies in the land. He used their enemies as part of His sovereign plan to test and to teach them. As you reflect on your life you may see some undeserved enemies in your land. Know that the Lord left them there as a teaching and training tool. They will not destroy you but push you onward towards maturity.

God saw a need to teach and train Israel's younger generation for war, because they were without battle experience. However, even in their training, He knew which nations would come up against Israel. He orchestrated the manner in which the various battles would take place. Their enemies were hand chosen by God for a specific purpose. Likewise, God knows the training you need, therefore; He has orchestrated the events in your life for a purpose. He will not allow the enemy to destroy you. God's purpose is greater and mightier than those of the devil. He's more concerned in bringing you into maturity and helping you to grow your faith.

As you reflect over the events (tests) in your life, how are you responding? Are you remaining faithful and trusting that God will pull you through?

Are you rebelling against God? Are you in a situation of rebellion and need to repent so you can return to fellowship? Have you humbled yourself before God and cried out to Him for deliverance? Or are you still holding on to the hurt, bitterness, and confusion? Can you display love in the midst of your furnace?

> *Romans 12:17-21 (NKJV) ¹⁷ Repay no one evil for evil. Have regard for good things in the sight of all men. ¹⁸ If it is possible, as much as depends on you, live peaceably with all men. ¹⁹ Beloved, do not avenge yourselves, but rather give place to wrath; for it is written, "Vengeance is Mine, I will repay," says the Lord. ²⁰ Therefore "If your enemy is hungry, feed him; if he is thirsty, give him a drink; for in so doing you will heap coals of fire on his head." ²¹ Do not be overcome by evil, but overcome evil with good.*

Let us not complain about the evil that has been done to us, it changes nothing. The more you respond to evil with evil the more evil increases. Repay no one evil for evil; instead do all YOU can to live peaceably. Do not avenge yourselves, for vengeance is mine, says the Lord. He will handle the situation; you keep doing what's right, keep on loving. Choose to forgive; don't allow bitterness to take root in your heart. Forgiving others will break the cycle of retaliation and lead to reconciliation. It frees you from the heavy load of bitterness. Let us overflow with love. Let us love beyond limits, don't allow the selfish acts of others to stop you from loving them like Christ loves you.

Overcome evil with good. **Overcome: is to mightily prevail over, to master, to be victorious.** In every situation you have a choice to either be a victor or a victim. God has placed on the inside of you the power to overcome evil with good. He wants you to experience His life in all of its abundance. *Romans 8:37 (NKJV) Yet in all these things we are more than conquerors through Him who loved us.* You are already a conqueror through Christ, now thank God for making you a conqueror over sin, over human desires, and over evil, through the power of Christ who lives within you. *Genesis 50:20 (MSG) Don't you see, you planned evil against me but God used those same plans for my good.* Refuse to be overwhelmed by what you are up against. Don't allow your emotions, burdens or excessive negative thinking to get the best of you. The power of Christ is greater than any opposition you may face. God meant it for your good and you shall mightily prevail over evil with good. Despite **"Love 10"** make a decision to display royal love for you are more than a conqueror and you can overcome all things in Jesus name.

Our love for one another must be unconditional. Let us learn to love each other like the father loves us. Can you love me despite what I am and what I am going through?

Prayer: On today, I choose to love my enemies, and I choose to forgive them and to let go of all bitterness, hatred, and frustration. I am not affected by their words; I release all bitterness and resentment now in the name of Jesus. As one of the forgiven, I now choose to forgive _____. I forgive every individual who has lied to me, stolen from me, robbed me of my innocence due to rape, abuse or molestation; anyone who has mistreated me, walked out on me, or plotted evil against me. I release my love one who has been unfaithful and deceiving. Lord, turn their hearts to you. I plead the blood of Jesus over my conscious mind and against the things that have been used by the enemy to keep me in bondage, depression, stress and anxiety. I thank you Lord that I will not rehearse any longer their evil actions. I have a royal mindset. I am delivered. I am free. I am healed. I am whole, and I am healthy! Lord I thank you for restoration, and I commit myself to serve you and love your people all the days of my life, in Jesus' name. Amen.

REFLECT AND JOURNAL:

Chapter 4

ANOINTED TO RULE WELL

Christians are anointed to carry out God's work on earth. Jesus Christ is your example of one who was found ruling well in His work for God's kingdom. As kings and priests of Jesus Christ you are indeed royalty. There is a measure of anointing that Christ has given each one of you in which He allows the anointing to assist you in ruling well. You shall represent Christ, act in His name and be accountable unto Him. As you stand in the position to rule, operating in your anointing, it brings growth, increase, and expansion in your life.

> *2 Samuel 23:1-4 (NKJV) ¹Now these are the last words of David. Thus says David the son of Jesse; ² "The Spirit of the LORD spoke by me, and His word was on my tongue. ³ The God of Israel said The Rock of Israel spoke to me: 'He who rules over men must be just, ruling in the fear of God. ⁴And he shall be like the light of the morning when the sun rises, a morning without clouds, like the tender grass springing out of the earth, by clear shining after rain.'*

David voiced God's expectations for rulers; they must be just, balanced, and stable. This is mandatory, not optional, for unjust rulers will create instability. Those who rule well He likened them to the light of the morning when the sun rises. They shall be like the tender grass springing out of the earth by the rain. As the earth sends forth rain, it causes growth. One who rules well will cause growth and increase in the land. They are visionary and are able to see past all barriers and believe things can flourish. They have the ability to decree a thing on earth, which causes growth and increase in the lives of God's people.

Job 22:28 (AMP) *"You shall also decide and decree a thing, and it shall be established for you; and the light [of God's favor] shall shine upon your ways."* ***Proverbs 18:21 (NIV)*** There's power in your words! *"Words kill, words give life; they're either poison or fruit – you choose."* When a king gives a decree, it is carried out as he decreed it. You have been given authority to rule and reign by the power of your words. You are heirs and joint-heirs with Jesus Christ. You were created to rule and reign and speak forth decrees upon the earth.

As you decide what you want your life to look like, start believing and decreeing it as the king that you are! Just as God spoke the world into existence, use your words to speak and decree your world into existence. Open your mouth, fill it with good words. Decree your victorious future and watch it manifest before your eyes!

Ruling well requires a measure of understanding. Understanding your times and seasons will help prevent you from making future mistakes, wrong turns, and unwise decisions. If you understand the season you are in then you will know if it's the right time for you to make a move. Some people run ahead of their season not discerning the timing of a thing. As a result, they end up feeling defeated, depleted, weary, and distressed. There is a set time and a set season for everything that God has for your life. ***Ecclesiastes 3:17(NKJV)*** declares it this way: ***There is a time for every purpose and for every work*** God has given everything on this earth a time to produce, to flourish, and a time to die.

> ***Ecclesiastes 3:1-8 (NKJV)*** *¹ To everything there is a season, a time for every purpose under heaven: ² A time to be born, and a time to die; a time to plant, and a time to pluck what is planted; ³ A time to kill, and a time to heal; a time to break down, and a time to build up; ⁴ A time to weep, and a time to laugh; a time to mourn, and a time to dance; ⁵ A time to cast away stones, and a time to gather stones; a time to embrace, and a time to refrain from embracing; ⁶ A time to gain, and a time to lose; a time to keep, and a time to throw away; ⁷ A time to tear, and a time to sew; a time to keep silence, and a time to speak; ⁸ A time to love, and a time to hate; a time of war, and a time of peace.*

Seasons last for a period of time. God said there is a time for every purpose under heaven. Learn to rule well in the midst of your season. Spending time in the word and in prayer prepares your spirit to discern the prompting and voice of God. God will not speak over your chaos and the noise around you. You must see and hear with your spiritual eyes and ears. Press into God and hear His voice, listen attentively to Him.

Are you in the planting or plucking season? Be mindful of what you plant in your life and the lives of others. When you are transitioning into new seasons do not fear change. This could make the move a more trying and confusing experience. Failing to move in God's timing can bring unwanted consequences, strained relationships, financial loss, and stress. You need to discern the times and seasons you're in and move with the Holy Spirit.

A farmer is able to rule well when he coordinates his activities according to the four seasons of the year. He knows the season for breaking up the ground, planting, reaping, harvesting and resting. Just as a farmer is knowledgeable about his activities in the proper season, we have a God who's more knowledgeable about the seasons in our life. Therefore; you must understand your times and seasons. If you are in a winter season and there does not seem to be any fruit appearing in your life, don't try to force it. You cannot produce fruit out of season. For it is God who produces fruit in you causing increase and expansion.

In every season, staying in touch with God is essential. Lot's wife missed her opportunity for deliverance because she turned around and looked back. Instead of moving straight ahead with the new plans God had for her life, she looked back at all that she was leaving behind. As a result, she lost her life. You cannot move from one season to the next with your eyes and mind always looking at your past. Ruling well requires a focused life, looking ahead towards what lies next for you and your family. One season of lost, pain or lack does not guarantee that this will be the same for your next season. Just as in the natural, we have four seasons and they are forever changing, so does the events in your life. I pause to present a question to you . . . . .

- Do you allow your dry seasons to hinder your next season by hanging on to the past or do you freely flow with your various seasons?

_____

_____

_____

_____

You need to recognize the season you're in and move forward!

Praying in every season is essential. *Ephesians 6:18 (NKJV) Praying always with all prayer and supplication in the Spirit...* Whether you are in a good season or a bad season, whether the opportunity seems to be favorable or unfavorable, by continually praying in the Spirit you will create the opportunity for God to illuminate your inner man with the knowledge you need to live circumspectly in the seasons of God. Always remain teachable and open to the seasons of new revelation that comes from the Holy Spirit.

As spoken earlier *Ecclesiastes 3:1(NKJV) To everything there is a season, a time for every purpose under heaven.* God's seasonal plan includes periods of growth and periods of rest. Recognizing the season you're in and responding appropriately to that season, is the best way to insure continued spiritual growth and a life that bears Godly fruit. Learn to be content and comfortable with the season that God has ordained for you.

When seasons come in your life, you must understand the purposes and plans of God, He will never do anything just to have something to do. All is planned and appointed for the proper times and seasons. He has already given you everything you need to be the seasonal plant you need to be in any season you may find yourself in.

> *Psalms 16:7(AMP) I will bless the Lord, who has given me counsel; yes, my heart instructs me in the night seasons*

Prayer: Thank you Lord for various times and seasons. We understand that we have authority to rule well on earth. Ecclesiastes 3:14 lets us know that "Whatever God does it shall be forever. Nothing can be added to it and nothing can be taken from it." So Lord we thank you because your work is of a durable quality and no one can undo it. It's final!

We give thanks in our season when there is no harvest because we understand that our harvest is coming. We understand that our seasons have a purpose divinely created by you. Thank you for helping me to lift up my head and move onward to my next season as I lean not on my own understanding but continue to acknowledge You and You will direct my path. I will embrace the seasons as they come and rule well in the midst of them, for I have been anointed to rule well in Jesus' name. Amen!

REFLECT AND JOURNAL:

Chapter 5

BREAKTHROUGH MANIFESTATION

Often times in life we go through a number of battles, and we are confronted with many difficult situations. However, in all that you may go through or experience, remember your breakthrough is near. We must learn to grasp the intended purpose behind difficult situations. God allows things to happen in our midst for a purpose, and *it's all working for your good according to Romans 8:28.* God has your breakthrough plan laid out before Him.

Breakthrough is the act of breaking through an obstacle or restriction. It's a sudden mark of change.

The things you are currently experiencing will not be your end. With each fiery dart from the enemy, remember who you are. You are of God and will overcome Satan. You have the shield of faith and you will quench every fiery dart that the wicked one brings against you and your household. I declare this is a brand new day in your life and no weapon fashioned against you shall succeed.

You shall overcome because God has given you the ability to stop Satan in his tracks. *Psalm 18:29 (NKJV) "For by You I have run through a troop: by my God I can leap over a wall."* It's time to run through the troops (those opposing forces) and to leap over the walls (those things that appear to have a permanent and solid dwelling). We see here that the psalmist was able to overcome the obstacles with God's help. The wall/troop is a natural thing but yet a difficult obstacle. How many of you are facing or dealing with a situation that is a natural thing but yet a difficult obstacle in your life? Odds are stacked against you, but God is able to breakthrough in our experience into the natural realm and help us to overcome difficulties. You may have been dealing with your situation for some time now, nevertheless as children of God we must understand it is not God's way to always immediately remove our walls, but instead He empowers us to leap over them. So despite what it looks like, your day of breakthrough is here, its NOW!

He gives us the power and strength to do what we cannot do on our own. Therefore, you will not grow weary while doing good, for in due season we shall reap if we do not lose heart. *Galatians 6:9 (NKJV)* I declare and decree in your life right now:

- That you are empowered by God to subdue and to exercise dominion.
- That every agent acting against your breakthrough be permanently paralyzed as God dismantles and destroys all power working against your life.
- As you run through the troops and leap over walls, the power of God shall blast forth mightily in your life, and He shall convert your defeat into triumph.
- That every difficulty, obstacle, wall, and prison is broken down and broken through in the name of Jesus.

I declare that victory is yours and the gates of hell shall not prevail against you. God will deliver you from the snare of the fowler. Despite what you are dealing with, you serve a God who is able to deliver his seed. Once in David's life when he was in the midst of trouble he began to speak what he saw, stading before him. Even though David was well aware of God's power at this particular point in his life he had a faith breakdown. However, he did not remain in this place. So regardless of where you are right now, I want you to know breakthrough time is now. It's not over for you or your seed. I don't care what the devil has told you, it is not over!

1 Samuel 27:1(NKJV) "But David thought to himself, "One of these days I will be destroyed by the hand of Saul. The best thing I can do is to escape to the land of the Philistines. Then Saul will give up searching for me anywhere in Israel, and I will slip out of his hand." David allowed discouragement to get in his heart, and he began to speak defeat. Whatever you may be experiencing do not allow discouragement to get in your heart. Make a reflection on the words you are giving voice to. When discouragement gets in your heart, it will mess with your mind and bring you to a place of breakdown and frustration. David gave voice to what was dwelling in his heart. **He said, *"Now I shall perish some day by the hand of Saul."*** Saul was David's opposing enemy, and he persecuted David on a continual basis. He was constantly and persistently seeking to take his life, this is known as the wear out tactics of the enemy. He keeps trying to wear you out in an attempt to break you down. But instead, you shall break out of every kingdom that stands opposed to the kingdom of God.

David voiced, *"Now I shall perish some day by the hand of Saul."* To perish is to die in a violent or untimely manner. How many have given in to the enemy because of weariness, frustration, and discouragement? David was speaking from where he was standing at that point in his life. We often speak from where we are standing at a certain point in life. The enemy wants nothing more than to break you down. But not today, your breakthrough manifestation is now! Lord manifest sudden breakthrough with overwhelming force which causes our enemies to turn. You will not perish by the hand of your enemy, but instead breakthrough the obstacles and walls.

Then David goes on to say, *"There is nothing better for me than that I should speedily escape to the land of the Philistines."* Have you ever got to a place in life and felt there is nothing better for you? So you devised a plan to escape. A plan that excluded the Lord, a plan that you thought was your only option. In David's attempt to escape to the land of the Philistines, the land of more enemies did not make sense. David wanted to escape from his enemy Saul because in his mind Saul seemed bigger than his enemy in the land of the Philistines.

Let us not devise a plan of escape in our minds but rely on the power of God. He can give you an escape route to better fit your needs. Cast your cares on him; release the obstacle over to the Lord. David felt in his mind this was the perfect escape, because Saul would not seek after him anymore. David wanted to run away from the enemy instead of just leaping over the wall- the problem. If God did not ordain the current escape route in your life then you are headed in the wrong direction. Don't allow the enemy to destroy your hope or to cause you to give in and have a breakdown.

You cannot let the enemy win; refuse to allow him to destroy your hope. Giving up, giving in, and discouragement will stop your breakthrough. Tell the devil that you are not going to have a breakdown! You will not give in to defeat. Today is the day of your breakthrough manifestation. **You are breaking out of:**

- Your prison mentality which has caused you to limit God's possibilities in your life.
- Spiritually laziness, living beneath your privileges.
- The spirit of control and manipulation from toxic relationships.
- The spirit of lack and feeling inadequate.
- The spirit of jealousy and fear.
- The spirit of rejection and depression.
- The spirit of heaviness and sickness.
- That adulterous relationship and those sexual sins.

I declare that by the reason of the anointing every yoke in your life is broken, in Jesus' name. You are coming out; I declare in this season that you are coming out of debt, poverty, shame, hopelessness, and helplessness in the name of Jesus. No longer will you be held captive by the enemy of your mind. No longer will you keep the door wide open for the enemy to attack. It's time to break out of hurt from the past, let it go. Break out from what they said and what they think let it go! Your breakthrough manifestation is here, no more restrictions or limitations!

> *Micah 2:12-13 (NIV)* *12 "I will surely gather all of you, Jacob; I will surely bring together the remnant of Israel. I will bring them together like sheep in a pen, like a flock in its pasture; the place will throng with people. 13 The One who breaks open the way will go up before them; they will break through the gate and go out. Their King will pass through before them, the Lord at their head."*

(Insert your name) when God makes you a promise it's a done deal. Regardless of what's going on in your life you need to know a promise is a promise. The first part of the promise made by the Lord to his people was to gather all of us together, like sheep in a pen. No matter where we have been scattered, He will gather the mass of people together and break open the way. You will move from your depression to freedom. It's time to come out! Your breakthrough manifestation is here; now walk in your freedom!

No longer will you allow the devil to stop you from walking in your freedom. When you receive your breakthrough manifestation you lay a course for others to follow. When you get free others will be set free. All difficulties will be removed and your pathway will be made clear. Right now you are moving from captivity to the place of promise = **Breakthrough Manifestation**. The supernatural power of God is breaking through every obstacle in your life and this is where you will begin to meet God in a new way, no longer feeling trapped in a narrow place. The breaker's anointing has been set in motion in your life. By the authority of the breaker's anointing, I declare breakthrough atmosphere to establish in your life, in your home, on your job, and in your ministry. You are breaking through all satanic barriers, demonic blockages, emotional barriers, spiritual barriers, and financial barriers in Jesus name.

God is at work in your life right now, but you have a real enemy who is trying to restrict you as he coils around you to tighten his grip trying to get you to shut down in the middle of your breakthrough. He knows this is your turning point, so he wants to shut you down! Yes you are frustrated, but this is your turning point. Doctors gave you some bad news, but this is your turning point. You are discouraged and depressed, but this is your turning point.

You must understand there are evil spirits that are standing against your breakthrough, and I sever every demonic activity designed to frustrate the purpose of God for your life. I loose you from all evil attachment, affliction, and association. Every internal power assigned against your breakthrough must die in the name of Jesus. You shall be free!

I call forth God's breaking anointing to shake up, move out, and be released in your life. You shall be free in the name of Jesus. Every power assigned against your breakthrough manifestation, your time is up, die in the name of Jesus. You will no longer be held in captivity – breakthrough manifestation is here! Today is your day of breakthrough in the name of Jesus.

- I decree doors of opportunity that have been closed in your life to be open now.
- I decree every demonic drought, famine, and recession ends now in the name of Jesus.
- I command your spiritual and financial climate to shift in the name of Jesus.
- No more lack, no more failure in the name of Jesus.
- I command every mountain in your way to move in the name of Jesus.
- Financial and emotional mountain move in the name of Jesus.
- Mountain of poverty, lack, and insufficiency move.
- Mountains of sickness, disease, and affliction move in the name of Jesus.

Breakthrough manifestation is here, you are free, and you are delivered!

God is King and has sovereign power and authority over the entire universe. *Isaiah 42:6-7 (NIV)* **⁶ "I, the LORD, have called you in righteousness; I will take hold of your hand. I will keep you and will make you to be a covenant for the people and a light for the Gentiles, ⁷ to open eyes that are blind, to free captives from prison and to release from the dungeon those who sit in darkness.**

The Lord has called you into righteousness and has given you instructions. You shall be a light to open the eyes that are blind with the truth of the Word, to free captives from prison and release from the dungeon those who sit in darkness. The Lord has partnered with me to let **you** know He has **something better for you.** *(Insert your name)* have you unlocked your power through the anointing and favor of God on your life? It's time for **you** to get in position, get in line with the call to live holy and serve God.

I declare everything is coming together:

- Your finances, your business, your vision for your life, its all coming together.
- Your children shall be released to succeed and fulfill their destiny.
- Your marriage/relationships shall be released from the hand of the enemy – its coming together.
- Your money is being released right now in the name of Jesus.
- Your breakthrough has been released.

I declare you have the victory in Jesus name! Breakthrough manifestation is here, now walk in your freedom!

REFLECT AND JOURNAL:

_____
_____
_____
_____
_____
_____
_____
_____
_____
_____
_____
_____
_____
_____
_____
_____
_____
_____
_____
_____
_____
_____
_____
_____
_____
_____
_____
_____
_____
_____
_____
_____
_____
_____
_____

Chapter 6

MOVING AWAY FROM DISTRACTIONS

Hebrews 12:1-2(NIV) [1] *Let us throw off anything that hinders and the sin that so easily entangles. And let us run with perseverance the race marked out for us,* [2] *fixing our eyes on Jesus, the pioneer and perfecter of faith.*

Distraction: is anything which takes a person's attention away from something else, to divert.

Every distraction comes with a purpose and you must be wise when distractions come your way. Have you allowed anything to draw your attention away from the plans and purposes that God has for your life? There will come a time when God requires a moving away from that which diverts your attention because of your gifting and abilities.

Our opening verse tells us to throw off, which means to release, to get rid of anything that hinders and all sin that entangles us. It's time to get rid of all distractions. No longer will you allow distractions or sin to pull you away from the plan God has designed specifically for you. I speak to your spirit now, no more entanglement, no more confusion!

- You will not be overtaken by evil work (distractions) *for the Lord shall deliver you from every evil work 2 Timothy 4:18 (NKJV).*
- You will not be oppressed by cares, difficulties and troubles; for you shall *cast all of your cares upon Him, for He cares for you 1 Peter 5:7 (NKJV).*

- You are not bound, for *the Son has made you free John 8:36 (NKJV)*.
- You are not defeated, for *you are more than a Conqueror through Christ who loves you Romans 8:37(NKJV)*.
- You are not weak, for *the Lord will give His angels strength over you to keep you Psalm 91:11(NKJV)*.
- You shall not lack any good thing for the Lord has promised *no good thing will He withhold from those who walk uprightly Psalm 84:11(NKJV)*.

In the life of Abram when the Lord began to reveal the plan and the promise to him, Abram was required to do something. The promise did not manifest overnight simply because the Lord spoke it. It took time for the promise to manifest. The Lord had to first move Abram away from distractions. *Genesis 12:1-5(NKJV)* *¹ Now the LORD had said to Abram: "Get out of your country, from your family and from your father's house, to a land that I will show you.² I will make you a great nation; I will bless you and make your name great; and you shall be a blessing. ³ I will bless those who bless you, and I will curse him who curses you; and in you all the families of the earth shall be blessed." ⁴ So Abram departed as the LORD had spoken to him, and Lot went with him. And Abram was seventy-five years old when he departed from Haran. ⁵ Then Abram took Sarai his wife and Lot his brother's son, and all their possessions that they had gathered, and the people whom they had acquired in Haran, and they departed to go to the land of Canaan.*

The Lord's plan will not always be comfortable; will not always be something you willingly jump to do, but it will always bring blessings in your life if you follow Him totally and completely. Let us not be distracted with our age, race, size or color but let us throw out every diversion that the devil tries to sow in your mind. Release it and move with the Lord. Satan is very good in positioning distractions in our way as we move towards the plans God has for us. Remember *Hebrews 12:1-2 (NKJV)* *¹ Let us throw off anything that hinders and the sin that so easily entangles us. ² Let us fix our eyes on Jesus, the author and finisher of our faith.*

As Abram packed up his things to go in the direction of the Lord he also packed up a distraction and took it with him. One must be very careful when moving away from distractions as a result of the voice of the Lord. You must know who and what should be going with you when moving in the direction that God called you to.

> *Genesis 13:1-9 (NKJV) ¹ Then Abram went up from Egypt, he and his wife and all that he had, and Lot with him, to the South ² Abram was very rich in livestock, in silver, and in gold. ³ And he went on his journey from the South as far as Bethel, to the place where his tent had been at the beginning, between Bethel and Ai, ⁴ to the place of the altar which he had made there at first. And there Abram called on the name of the LORD.⁵ Lot also, who went with Abram, had flocks and herds and tents. ⁶ Now the land was not able to support them, that they might dwell together, for their possessions were so great that they could not dwell together. ⁷ And there was strife between the herdsmen of Abram's livestock and the herdsmen of Lot's livestock. The Canaanites and the Perizzites then dwelt in the land.⁸ So Abram said to Lot, "Please let there be no strife between you and me, and between my herdsmen and your herdsmen; for we are brethren. ⁹ Is not the whole land before you? Please separate from me. If you take the left, then I will go to the right; or, if you go to the right, then I will go to the left.*

As Abram continued on his journey with his wife and nephew Lot, the hand of God was at work. The land was not able to support them to dwell together, therefore; Abram and Lot had to separate. God was working something on behalf of Abram's promise. God had a plan specifically designed for Abram, therefore; he could not take everyone with him to receive his promise. *Genesis 13:14-17 (NKJV) ¹⁴ And the LORD said to Abram, after Lot had separated from him: "Lift your eyes now and look from the place where you are—northward, southward, eastward, and westward; ¹⁵ for all the land which you see I give to you and your descendants forever. ¹⁶ And I will make your descendants as the dust of the earth; so that if a man could number the dust of the earth, then your descendants also could be numbered. ¹⁷ Arise, walk in the land through its length and its width, for I give it to you."*

After the separation the Lord spoke to **Abram** concerning his promise. He said," Look, for ALL that you see I will give to you and your descendants." In other words, you will know that the Lord has blessed you indeed. He had an awesome plan for Abram's household. Even in your life, refuse to be distracted by family and love ones, release them and let them go. Continue to love them but don't be afraid to let them go. They may not understand, but you must let them go in order to receive the blessing, which God has for you in this season. Despite how you feel obey the voice of the Lord, it will work for your good. Now obey and move on!

> *Genesis 15:1-5 (NKJV) ¹ After these things the word of the LORD came to Abram in a vision, saying, "Do not be afraid, Abram. I am your shield, your exceedingly great reward." ² But Abram said, "Lord GOD, what will You give me, seeing I go childless, and the heir of my house is Eliezer of Damascus?" ³ Then Abram said, "Look, You have given me no offspring; indeed one born in my house is my heir!" ⁴ And behold, the word of the LORD came to him, saying, "This one shall not be your heir, but one who <u>will come from your own body shall be your heir</u>." ⁵ Then He brought him outside and said, "Look now toward heaven, and count the stars if you are able to number them." And He said to him, "So shall your descendants be."*

God again speaks to Abram about the promise and Abram looking with his natural eyes could not see how it would come to pass, being that he was childless. God goes on to reassure Abram of the things to come *He brought him outside and said, "Look now toward heaven, and count the stars if you are able to number them." And He said to him, "So shall your descendants be."* In other words, I got this Abram, I know what I'm doing, and the heir shall come from your own body in my timing. You must understand that there is a process before the promise. The Lord repeatedly spoke about the promise but Abram had to go through his process before the promise could manifest. I encourage you not to give up during the process. If God has indeed spoken a promise to you, then don't you dare give up during the process. God is stirring you within. The promise is coming!

So during the process of time Abram gave ear to his wife and her suggestions. Now *Genesis 16:1-4 (NKJV) ¹ Sarai, Abram's wife, had borne him no children. And she had an Egyptian maidservant whose name was Hagar. ² So Sarai said to Abram, "See now, the LORD has restrained me from bearing children. Please, go in to my maid; perhaps I shall obtain children by her." And Abram heeded the voice of Sarai. ³ Then Sarai, Abram's wife, took Hagar her maid, the Egyptian, and gave her to her husband Abram to be his wife, after Abram had dwelt ten years in the land of Canaan. ⁴ So he went in to Hagar, and she conceived. And when she saw that she had conceived, her mistress became despised in her eye.*

Yet another distraction! This was a plan to make things happen. Abram acted outside of God's plan. He did not tell Abram to sleep with Hagar. Be careful of distractions while you are going through your process. When God speaks to you about your promise while waiting on manifestation, simply obey God. You do not have to try to make things happen, this is what we call a ___distraction___, to divert you from God's original plan. Have you allowed something to divert your attention away from God's original plan for your life? Somebody is going through their process and has allowed a distraction to lead them astray. God wants you to release it and let it go! What He has promised it shall come to past. Release, repent, and move on!

After the process of time; God spoke again to Abram *Genesis 17:1-8, 15-22 (NKJV) ¹ When Abram was ninety-nine years old, the LORD appeared to Abram and said to him, "I am Almighty God; walk before Me and be blameless. ² And I will make My covenant between Me and you, and will ___multiply you exceedingly___." ³ Then Abram fell on his face, and God talked with him, saying: ⁴ "As for Me, behold, My covenant is with you, and you shall be a father of many nations. ⁵ No longer shall your name be called Abram, but your name shall be Abraham; for I have made you a father of many nations. ⁶ I will make you ___exceedingly fruitful___; and I will make* *nations of you, and kings shall come from you. ⁷ And I will establish My covenant between Me and you and your descendants after you in their generations, for an everlasting covenant, to be God to you and your descendants after you. ⁸ Also I give to you and your descendants after you the land in which you are a stranger, all the land of Canaan, as an everlasting possession; and I will be their God." ¹⁵ Then God said to Abraham, "As for Sarai your wife, you shall not call her name Sarai, but Sarah shall be her name. ¹⁶ And I will bless her and also give you a son by her; then I will bless her, and <u>she shall be a mother of nations; kings of peoples shall be from her.</u>"¹⁷ Then Abraham fell on his face and laughed, and said in his heart, "Shall a child be born to a man who is one hundred years old? And shall Sarah, who is ninety years old, bear a child?" ¹⁸ And Abraham said to God, "Oh, that Ishmael might live before You!"¹⁹ <u>Then God said: "No, Sarah your wife shall bear you a son, and you shall call his name Isaac; I will establish My covenant with him for an everlasting covenant, and with his descendants after him.</u> ²⁰ And as for Ishmael, I have heard you. Behold, I have blessed him, and will make him fruitful, and will multiply him exceedingly. He shall beget twelve princes, and I will make him a great nation. ²¹ But My covenant I will establish with Isaac, whom Sarah shall bear to you at this set time next year." ²² Then He finished talking with him, and God went up from Abraham.*

God began once again to talk to Abram about the promise. He said, "He would multiply him exceedingly, he would be exceedingly fruitful, make nations and kings to come from him." All this was to take place in God's timing. Despite what Abram saw, God spoke words of life, hope and blessings. As a matter of fact, he was going to be a father of many nations. Therefore, He would change his name to Abraham. As for Sari your wife, "She shall be called the mother of nations, kings of people shall be from her." God was determined that the seed, the child of heir was to be born of Sarah and his name shall be called Isaac, and He was going to multiply him as well. God had a plan for this family. He spoke it into existence, and He did not allow man, woman, or age, to change His plan. So as you think about what God has spoken to you, don't you dare allow anyone, or anything to change what God has spoken.

God gave Abram the complete package for the promise and what was to come. ***Genesis 21:1-3 (NKJV) ¹ And the LORD visited Sarah as He had said, and the LORD did for Sarah as He had spoken. ² For Sarah conceived and bore Abraham a son in his old age, at the set time of which God had spoken to him. ³ And Abraham called the name of his son who was born to him—whom Sarah bore to him—Isaac.***

God's promise to make Abraham's descendants into a great nation was fulfilled in Abraham's life at the set time. It was through the birth of Isaac and then later Jacob, through whom the twelve tribes of Israel were born, that Abraham's descendants did indeed become a great nation. God promised Abraham that ***"Through him every family on earth will be blessed" Genesis 12:3.***

- Abraham had two sons (Ishmael and Isaac)
- Isaac had two sons (Esau/Jacob)
- Jacob had twelve sons (Reuben, Simeon, Levi, Judah, Issachar, Zebulun, Gad, Asher, Dan, Naphtali, Joseph and Benjamin)
- Judah father of David and Jesus Christ

Despite all distractions Abraham faced, he had to release them and keep moving in the direction of the Lord. As he did, he prospered and God's plans for his life came to pass. You cannot afford to allow distractions or sin to entangle you or to keep you from your promises. It's time to move away from distractions.

In your life the devil will offer you things that he knows will grab your attention. He is trying to divert your attention away from God. You must continue to rebuke the devil, do not eat his bait, throw it off, refuse it, and do not accept it! Jesus refused the devil when he came to tempt Him in Matthew 4:1-11, you must do likewise. Jesus refused to settle for serving anyone or anything less than God himself. Have you made up your mind as to whom you will serve? It's time to move away from distractions! Satan will use any method he can to get your attention off of the things of God making it appear as if it's the best possible situation for you. ***1 Peter 5:8 (NKJV) Be sober, be vigilant; because your adversary the devil walks about like a roaring lion,***

seeking whom he may devour. Keep your eyes focused on Jesus, the author and finisher of your faith!

Stop accepting distractions of the devil, resist him and he will flee. Take authority over Satan and break the power of any evil that has been spoken over your life. All the forces of darkness have no power to affect your body. I cast down and break the power of any strategies, maneuvers, or evil plots that the enemy has set in motion to bring destruction to your life. They shall all come to naught because no weapon formed against (Insert your name) will prosper in Jesus name! Satan, in Jesus name I disarm you. I bring down all your strongholds and proud pretensions (2 Corinthians 10:4-5). I cast you out in Jesus' name. You shall walk in the authority you have been given over demons (Matthew 10:1) in Jesus name. Amen.

I say this once again; stop allowing distractions to push you outside of God's plans. Distractions can carry you further than you ever intended to go in a particular direction. It diverts you to other paths all the while taking you further and further away from the Lord's presence. Just as Jonah made the decision to run away from the presence of the Lord in the opposite direction; he too ended up way out there. He ended up in a place he had no idea he would be. So shall you be if you continue on that path of disobedience. Stop allowing distractions to send you in the wilderness, living in the belly of a gruesome fish for day in and day out. Make the decision now to get it right, repent and get back on the right track. **You are one decision away from change**.

So many people really don't understand the simple but powerful concept of actually making a decision that will forever change their lives. You are only one decision away from changing and rerouting your path to success in God's kingdom. It all begins with making the one decision that starts it all. What's the one thing that's holding you back from where you want to go in life? It's time to let go of fear, things that you are emotionally connected to, those things that you are afraid to lose. Right now is your time for change. Stop wasting time over-thinking and over analyzing things, let go and simply step out on faith. Where would we be if Abraham was caught up in over thinking and never moving or advancing ahead to God's call? Remember, **you are one decision**

away from change. For some that one decision may be to make Jesus the Lord of their life.

Prayer: Heavenly Father, in the Name of Jesus, I present myself to You. I pray and ask Jesus to be Lord over my life. I believe it in my heart, so I say it with my mouth: Jesus has been raised from the dead. This moment, I make Him the Lord over my life. Jesus, come into my heart. I believe at this moment that I am saved. I say it now: I am reborn. I am a Christian. I am a child of Almighty God. Amen. **Scripture References: John 1:12; 3:16; 6:37; 10:10; John 14:6; John 16:8-9; Romans 3:23; Romans 5:8; Romans 10:9-10, 13; 2 Corinthians 5:1, 7, 19, 21.**

For others it may be to renew your commitment to the Lord, release your burdens, calm your anxious heart and still your troubling thoughts. I release my hands from those things that has held me bound, those things that I think is working for my good. I release it now in the name of Jesus. Lord with this decision of change may your complete will be done in my life. I surrender myself totally and completely to you, in Jesus name, Amen.

Lord, teach me to operate under your full power and authority so I will not allow distractions from my home, marriage, relationships, children, family or co workers to stop God's manifestations in my life.

- I release my home to you Lord.
- I release my marriage to you Lord.
- I release my relationship to you Lord.
- I release all of my family members to you Lord.
- I release my thinking to you Lord.
- I release my co-workers to you Lord.
- I release my ministry to you Lord.
- I release my _____ to you Lord.

Lord I release every distraction and hindrance to you!
Now make me better Lord, in Jesus name. Amen!

REFLECT AND JOURNAL:

Chapter 7

CHOSEN BY GOD TO REIGN

Romans 5:17 (NKJV)For if by one man's offense death reigned through the one, much more those who received abundance of grace and of the gift of righteousness will reign in life through the one, Jesus Christ.

You shall reign in life through Jesus Christ, the one who has all power and authority. Reign in this verse denotes the meaning to have kingly rule to possess kingly dominion. A king rules and reigns over his/her domain. Your domain includes all for which you have authority, influence and responsibility over. As a child of God you should reign over circumstances, relationships, finances, ministry, sickness and disease. God has positioned and called you to reign.

You were born of God for a specific purpose. You were chosen by God.
- **You have received the gift of righteousness and reign as a king in life by Jesus Christ - Romans 5:17 (NKJV).**
- **You are a joint-heir with Christ - Romans 8:17 (NKJV).**
- **You are an ambassador for Christ - 2 Corinthians 5:20 (NKJV).**

1 Peter 2:9 establishes your identity:
- **You are a chosen generation,**
- **A Royal Priesthood,**
- **A holy nation,**
- **A special (peculiar) people to declare His praises.**
- **You have been called out of darkness and placed into God's marvelous light!**

You have been chosen to reign! You have the power to:
- Take authority over sickness and demonic forces.
- Decree and declare God's word over you and your family.
- Reign over and crush a lifestyle of sin.
- Dream dreams and see visions from the Holy Spirit.
- Be the head and not the tail; above and not beneath.

The Lord reigns on this earth for He is the ruler of all eternity and through Him you shall reign as well. *Psalm 93:1(NKJV) says, "The Lord reigns, the Lord is clothed with majesty; He has girded Himself with strength." Isaiah 52:7(NKJV) Your God reigns.* Jesus is clothed with majesty; He is girded with strength and is able to withstand stress and to resist attack. He is dressed in garments of victory! Our God reigns! He controls every power on earth and has given that same power to those who have received Him. We must agree with His will and speak as one who reigns.

Before the foundation of the world you were chosen by God to reign on this earth. To be chosen means to be selected from or preferred above others (elect).

- *He chose us in Him before the foundation of the world - Ephesians 1:4 (NKJV).*
- *And we know that all things work together for good to those who love God, to those who are called according to His purpose - Romans 8:28 (NKJV).*
- *He has saved us and called us a holy calling, not according to our works, but according to His own purpose and grace which was given to us in Christ Jesus before time began - 2 Timothy 1:9 (NKJV).*

As stated in the scriptures above you were chosen and called before the foundation of the world and you had to agree with God's call. You were chosen in Him for His purpose before time began. You were chosen to reign!

Reign: is to exercise sovereignty powers, sovereignty rules. Reigning produces the abundant life.

Moses was chosen by God to reign but before he could actually reign in what God called him to do, he had to accept that he was chosen. God specifically picked him for a purpose greater than his current position (which was tending to his father-in-law's flock).

Exodus 3:1-8, 10, (NKJV) ¹ Now Moses was tending the flock of Jethro his father-in-law, the priest of Midian. And he led the flock to the back of the desert, and came to Horeb, the mountain of God. ² And the Angel of the Lord appeared to him in a flame of fire from the midst of a bush. So he looked, and behold, the bush was burning with fire, but the bush was not consumed. ³ Then Moses said, "I will now turn aside and see this great sight, why the bush does not burn." ⁴ So when the Lord saw that he turned aside to look, God called to him from the midst of the bush and said, "Moses, Moses!" And he said, "Here I am." ⁵ Then He said, "Do not draw near this place. Take your sandals off your feet, for the place where you stand is holy ground." ⁶ Moreover He said, "I am the God of your father—the God of Abraham, the God of Isaac, and the God of Jacob." And Moses hid his face, for he was afraid to look upon God. ⁷ And the Lord said: "I have surely seen the oppression of My people who are in Egypt, and have heard their cry because of their taskmasters, for I know their sorrows. ⁸ So I have come down to deliver them out of the hand of the Egyptians, and to bring them up from that land to a good and large land, to a land flowing with milk and honey, to the place of the Canaanites and the Hittites and the Amorites and the Perizzites and the Hivites and the Jebusites. ¹⁰ Come now, therefore, and I will send you to Pharaoh that you may bring My people, the children of Israel, out of Egypt."

He chose Moses for a royal task of leading his people out of bondage (Egypt). But before Moses could move forward, he had to come into agreement with what he was called to do. God was putting a demand on Moses to simply use what He placed within him before the foundation of the world.

Exodus 3:11- 13 (NKJV) [11] But Moses said to God, "Who am I that I should go to Pharaoh, and that I should bring the children of Israel out of Egypt?" [12] So He said, "I will certainly be with you. And this shall be a sign to you that I have sent you: When you have brought the people out of Egypt, you shall serve God on this mountain." [13] Then Moses said to God, "Indeed, when I come to the children of Israel and say to them, 'The God of your fathers has sent me to you,' and they say to me, 'What is His name?' what shall I say to them?"

As God gives Moses instructions for the task at hand we witness Moses' questions and God's response. Moses had to get acquainted with God. He said, "What shall I say when they ask me who sent me?"

Exodus 3:14-15 [14] And God said to Moses, "I AM WHO I AM." And He said, "Thus you shall say to the children of Israel, 'I AM has sent me to you.'" [15] Moreover God said to Moses, "Thus you shall say to the children of Israel: 'The LORD God of your fathers, the God of Abraham, the God of Isaac, and the God of Jacob, has sent me to you. This is My name forever, and this is My memorial to all generations.'

The Lord proceeded to give Moses clear cut instructions for what He was chosen to do. He called Moses out of darkness. It did not matter about Moses' experience, past or current position, the only thing that mattered to God was for Moses to simply go forth and do what He chose him to do. He gave Moses authority and influence over the Children of Israel, they were his domain and all he had to do was to reign.

I decree and declare in your life on today:

- That you are who God says that you are - a champion, a winner, a conqueror!
- You are a royal priesthood, a holy nation!
- You are strong and secure, you are royalty!
- Your life has meaning and you are full of potential!
- You will be all that God calls you to be in Jesus name, Amen!

REFLECT AND JOURNAL:

Chapter 8

UNLIMITED POSSIBILITIES

In God the possibilities are unlimited. *Psalm 147:5 (GWT) "Our Lord is great and his power is great. There is no limit to His understanding."*

Life is so full of challenges but with every challenge life brings before you there is a solution. We live in a world full of possibilities for our God has no limits. *Romans 4:20-21 (NKJV) " 20 Abraham did not waver at the promise of God through unbelief, but was strengthened in faith, giving glory to God 21 and being fully convinced that what He has promised He was able to perform."*

Abraham believed that God was able to do just what He said. He was fully convinced that what He promised He was able to perform. Are you convinced that with God the possibilities are unlimited? Do you believe that He is able to perform miracles? Do you understand that we serve a God full of possibilities?

Luke 1:37(NKJV) For with God nothing shall be impossible. The word impossible means not capable of being accomplished; extremely difficult to deal with or tolerate. So simply put. With God, impossible doesn't exist! Grab hold of this promise from *Luke 1:37 (NKJV) For with God nothing shall be impossible.* If it does not exist in God's kingdom, it should not exist in a child of God's life. No matter what you are facing, our God is not limited by it; He can do all things because He knows no limits. Nothing shall shake you or throw you off, refuse to believe the lies of the enemy. Grab hold of the promises of God! If you are facing discouragement, disappointment, depression or despair, will you believe that NOTHING will be IMPOSSIBLE with God? If you are struggling in your family/relationships, will you believe that NOTHING will be IMPOSSIBLE with God? Don't allow anyone to tell you what God can't do, there are no limits in God!

To turn what may look like an impossible situation around you must have faith in God. You must believe without a shadow of doubt that God can and will turn it around just for you. As you begin to speak God's word over your situation and believe what you are saying, manifestation will come. *Matthew 19:26 (NLT) Jesus looked at them intently and said, "Humanly speaking, it is impossible. But with God everything is possible."* Endless possibilities, no boundaries, infinite wisdom and strength! Miracles and healings, nothing will be impossible with God!

The God of impossibilities spared Moses life at birth. Before his birth: Pharaoh commanded all the people in *Exodus 1:22 (NKJV) Every son who is born you shall cast into the river and every daughter you shall save alive.* This was a command to kill all male babies by drowning them in a river, but guess what, Moses was born at this time when Pharaoh issued the command – and He did not lose his life, because God had purpose for him. No issue, decree or command can stop our God. There are no limits in God.

This same God has power to heal all manners of sickness. *Luke 22:49-51 (NKJV) ⁴⁹ When those around Him saw what was going to happen, they said to Him, "Lord, shall we strike with the sword?" ⁵⁰ And one of them struck the servant of the high priest and <u>cut off his right ear</u>.⁵¹ But Jesus answered and said, "Permit even this." And He touched his ear and healed him.*

You see Judas had just betrayed Jesus with a kiss and the men with him knew to seize the one he kissed. When those around Jesus realized what was happening they wanted to do something to prevent it from happening. But Jesus knew this thing that was about to take place had to happen. He saw what was yet to come.

So Peter, in an attempt to prevent it pulled out his sword and began to use it. He cut off the servant's right ear. You must see this for what it is, Peter cut off the servant's ear but look at the God of impossibilities. *Jesus said "permit even this" and He touched his ear and healed him!*

When you think about the ear being cut off it means it is no longer where it should be, it is gone, it has been removed. But it did not limit what God was able to do, He yet performed a miracle. This miracle took place outside in nature, we serve a God who has unlimited resources.

You see there was no washing his hands, gloves or surgical preparation or instruments. All he had was a word in His mouth and healing sprang forth! When you think about an ear being connected to the side of your head how things are aligned perfectly so one can hear. It's aligned with tubes inside for a purpose. You have the outer ear, middle ear and the inner ear but yet somehow, Jesus spoke a word and touched his ear and healing came attaching muscles, nerve endings, blood vessels and veins perfectly. He received his healing. In God the possibilities are unlimited. He is able to do all things. Do you believe God can work a miracle in your life? You must understand the power of God.

Proverbs 21:1 (NKJV) The king's heart is in the hand of the LORD, like the rivers of water; He turns it wherever He wishes. Our God is all powerful; He has authority in his hands. In God's hand the king's heart will be what thus says the Lord. In God's hands the rivers of water will flow in the direction of thus says the Lord. Even in God's hands your life will be what thus said the Lord. *2 Kings 13:14, 20-21 ¹⁴ Elisha had become sick with the illness of which he would die. ²⁰ Then Elisha died, and they buried him. And the raiding bands from Moab invaded the land in the spring of the year. ²¹ So it was, as they were burying a man, that suddenly they spied a band of raiders; and they put the man in the tomb of Elisha; and when the man was let down and touched the bones of Elisha, he revived and stood on his feet.* This man's life was revived. It showed God's demonstration of His power. It showed our God working in the midst of what looked like a limited situation. In this portion of text it does not say they were believing or praying for this man's life, no they were simply burying him because he was dead and his life was over. But by God's unlimited power He turned it around. We serve a God of unlimited possibilities.

Can you believe God for the miraculous? Can you believe God for your turn around in the midst of what looks hopeless? Can you believe God?

Prayer: *Psalm 147:5 (GWT) "Our Lord is great and his power is great. There is no limit to His understanding."* Lord because I believe there are no limits to what you know, I will walk in the fullness of all that you have for me. In you there are no limits, therefore, in me I shall not be limited, controlled or hindered. I will walk in faith and agree with God and live in the realm of possibility all the days of my life, in Jesus' name. Amen.

REFLECT AND JOURNAL:

Chapter 9

THUS SAYS THE LORD, YOU COMMAND ME

Isaiah 45:11-12 (NKJV) ¹¹ Thus says the Lord, The Holy One of Israel, and his Maker, "Ask Me of things to come concerning My sons; and concerning the work of My hands, you command Me. I have made the earth, and created man on it. I - my hands -stretched out the heavens, and all their host have I commanded."

Sometimes it may seem as though life is tossing you to and fro. You may feel like you have gotten a bad deal in this thing called life due to your circumstances. It may appear to look bad, as if things are not working out for you at all. It may seem as though you cannot get ahead, as though you are held in a certain location over a lengthy period of time. But despite what the facts may be you need to remember what thus says the Lord concerning his sons and the work of His hands. How He specifically tells you to command Him, for "***He knows the thoughts that He think toward you, (says the Lord), thoughts of peace and not of evil, to give you a future and a hope" Jeremiah 29:11, (NKJV).*** So regardless of how things may look or how long you have been in a certain location in life, the devil wants you to believe that this is as good as your life will ever get. He wants you to doubt the plans of God for your life. He wants you to live beneath what God has created for you. God's thoughts of you are for peace and not of evil, to give you a future and a hope. He wants you to live larger and to bring you into the good life He has created for you. It was His hands that stretched out this world and brought man (you and I) into it. So whatever you are in need of, seek Him for the plan.

The statement "Thus says the Lord," emphasizes the certainty that the statement will be fulfilled. If the Lord said it, shall it not be fulfilled? For *Numbers 23:19, (NKJV) God is not a man, that He should lie, nor a son of man, that He should repent. Has He said it, and will He not do it? Or has He spoken, and will He not make it good. Malachi 3:6 (NKJV) I am the Lord and I do not change...* Whatever the Lord has said or spoken He shall make it good, whether you believe him or not, He cannot lie! Whether you listen to Him or not, He does not change! What He calls forth in your life, no man can reverse or undo, they are powerless to change what God has blessed or declared to be blessed. God will not renege on His promises. *Romans 8:31 (NKJV) If God is for us, then who can be against us.* You must believe and declare the promises of God in your life.

"Thus says the Lord, You command me," for He knows the path and plans for your life. He wants you to command Him. *Isaiah 64:8 (NKJV) ...You are the Father: we are the clay, and You our potter; and all we are the works of Your hands.* We desire for you O Lord to have your perfect way in our life. We command your plan to come forth in every area of our life. We understand and know it was you O Lord who created us on this earth. And during that time of creation you knew the plan for our life and we seek you on today to call that plan forth to maturity in our life. We will be what you have created us to be, and we command it to be so now, in the name of Jesus.

It was with your hands that you stretched out the heavens and all their host - You commanded it! At your command, things came into existence, and you tell us to "...*call those things which be not as though they were, Romans 4:17 (KJV).* We must begin to speak of things as we want them to be. Our future is bright, and it is loaded with the promises of God. I decree and declare promotion, prosperity, a healthy life, debt freedom and God's favor in your life on today. I decree and declare that your relationships will be restored, healed, whole and free of debris. I decree and declare that you shall be all that God has created and called you forth to be. At your command Lord, *"A little one shall become a thousand and a small one a strong nation. I, the*

Lord, will hasten it in its time" Isaiah 60:22 (NKJV). In His time increase shall come forth in your life.

At His command, the blessings shall flow in your life. ***Deuteronomy 28:12-13 (NKJV)*** *[12] **The LORD will open to <u>you</u> his good treasure, <u>the heavens </u>to give the rain to your land in its season, and to bless <u>all</u> the work of <u>your </u>hand. <u>You</u> shall lend to many nations, but you shall not borrow. And the LORD will make <u>you</u> the head, and not the tail; <u>you</u> shall be above only, and not be beneath; <u>if you</u> heed the commandments of the LORD your God, which I command today, and are careful to observe them.*** He opens his good treasures unto us:

- He commands the blessing of rain on your land!
- He will bless all the work of your hand = increase, overflow, and more than enough!
- You shall lend to many nations and not borrow!
- You shall be the head and not the tail!
- You shall be above only and not beneath!
- All these things will be yours **if** you heed and observe the commandments of the Lord.

Heed: to give careful attention to, to regard.
Observe: to regard with attention, to see or learn something.

In order for these blessings to be so in your life you must do something. So if you heed and observe His commandments, then these things will be so in your life. Remember the word **if** brings a condition, requirement or stipulation with it. But if you choose not to heed and to observe His commandments, these things will not be so in your life. You must do something! ***Psalm 107:2 (NKJV) Let the redeemed of the Lord say so...*** There is a connection between what you say and what God does. When you speak the Word from within your spirit it then becomes life and brings results. We must learn to speak the Word from our spirit and not just as something to say or a fancy cliché. You must ***"Let the Word of Christ dwell in you richly in all wisdom..."*** ***Colossians 3:16 (NKJV).*** In other words let the Word of Christ live in you abundantly or extravagantly. When the word is living in you in this manner, it will lead you to a productive and prosperous place.

It will bring forth enormous and great prosperity because it's living in you. As you begin to speak the Word of Christ from your spirit it will bring forth life, healing, health and prosperity in your midst. As Mary began to speak from her spirit what she heard the angel of the Lord say, it brought forth prosperity and greatness upon the earth. Notice Mary could not speak what she was not in tune with the spirit to speak. She spoke it from her spirit and as a result gave birth to a powerful nation. So as you being to speak God's word from your spirit watch what God has put in you come to life. *Numbers 14:28 (NKJV) Just as you have spoken in My hearing, so I will do to you.*

Isaiah 45:11 (NKJV) Thus says the Lord, "Ask Me of things to come concerning My sons; and concerning the work of My hands, you command Me. God has a destiny and plan for your life, command Him for your destiny, call forth what He has already set aside for you. As you declare God's word in your life it will be so.

- *Proverbs 18:21 (KJV) Death and life are in the power of the tongue: and they that love it shall eat the fruit of thereof.*
- Start declaring a better future with your words: *Isaiah 46:10 (NKJV) Declaring the end from the beginning and from the ancient times things that are not yet done, saying, 'My counsel shall stand and I will do all My pleasure.'*
- *2 Corinthians 5:17 (NKJV) Therefore, if anyone is in Christ, he is a new creation; old things have passed away; behold, all things have become new.* Today is a brand new day in your life. Old cycles of failure, lost, and hurt are gone; you have new cycles of victory, success, and prosperity!
- *Mark 11:23 (NKJV) Whoever says to this mountain, 'Be removed and be cast into the sea,' and does not doubt in his heart, but believes that those things he says will be done, he will have whatever he says.* Speak to your mountain. You will have whatever you say.
- *Proverbs 13:22 (NKJV) A good man leaves an inheritance to his children's children, but the wealth of the sinner is stored up for the righteous.* I decree and declare that you will leave an inheritance for your children and your children's children.

With all of this being said, you need to continue to ***Isaiah 45:11 (NKJV) Ask Me of things to come concerning My sons; and concerning the work of My hands, <u>you</u> command Me.*** As you do, He shall bring those things He has for your life to past, and they shall come forth in your life!

REFLECT AND JOURNAL:

Chapter 10

THE ROYAL GOODNESS OF GOD

Psalm 65:4 (NKJV) Blessed is the man You choose, and cause to approach You, that he may dwell in Your courts. We shall be satisfied with the goodness of your house, of your holy temple.

Those in whom Christ laid down His life for shall dwell, abide and be in fellowship with Him. Happy is he, for God's goodness shall satisfy thee. He shall fulfill your desires, expectations and needs, daily with His goodness. There shall be no lack, but an ample and sufficient supply.

Psalm 65:9-13(NKJV) ⁹ You visit the earth and water it, You greatly enrich it; the river of God is full of water; You provide their grain, for so You have prepared it. ¹⁰ You water its ridges abundantly, You settle its furrows; You make it soft with showers, You bless its growth.¹¹ You crown the year with your goodness, and your paths drip with abundance. ¹² They drop on the pastures of the wilderness, and the little hills rejoice on every side. ¹³ The pastures are clothed with flocks; the valleys also are covered with grain; they shout for joy, they also sing.

Rainfall is seen as a visitation of God as it brings productivity to the earth. He did not show up empty handed when He visited the earth, He watered it and greatly enriched it. He gave out of His royal supply of goodness and the earth brought forth increase as He provided their grain in which He had prepared. He watered its ridges abundantly, gave it more than enough and it brought forth growth. The royal goodness of God shows that He blesses, He gives, He heals, He delivers and He provides. One of the Hebrew names for God is, Jehovah-Jireh, meaning "God the Provider." He sees what lies ahead and provides for it in advance.

He crowns the year with His goodness, to crown something denotes the meaning as: to be at the top or highest part of, to bring to a successful or triumphant conclusion. The Lord Himself sits at the top of this year (at the beginning) and He sits at the conclusion (at the end). He completely encircles it and provides for you everything you need.

God has crowned the year with goodness; He is not limited by time or space. He sits above the year from the highest point over everything that happens. He sees it all. *Proverbs 15:3 (NKJV) "The eyes of the Lord are in every place, keeping watch on the evil and the good."* And He will orchestrate and work things out for our good according to Romans 8:28. It did not say that all things are good, but He caused them to work together for the good. In the life of Joseph, he found himself in several bad situations, however in the end; they worked together for the good. He was thrown in the pit, sold into slavery by his brothers; he was later thrown into prison because of a lie told by the king's wife. These things were not good but yet God with his royal goodness brought good out of it. Joseph was able to help the nation of Israel because he was put in a place of authority in Egypt. You must remember when bad things happen to you, God knows how to work them together for your good. So whatever bad may come your way this year, you can expect to see God's goodness at work bringing things together to work for your good. He will transform your life; His goodness will work on your behalf.

He said your paths drip with abundance. When something drips, it's a continuous flow and can bring about an overflow of abundance. As I think about the word drip, it means to fall in drops. For example, the faucet is dripping, and it has the potential to overflow. The Word of God said, *"Your paths shall drip with abundance!"* He will bring prosperity to your life. This is abundance in every area of your life; it's an extreme plentiful or over sufficient quantity or supply. His abundance drops on the pastures of the wilderness and they are clothed with flocks, an overflow blessing. His abundance also allows the valley to be covered with grain; yielding an overflow of blessings.

Because of God's abundance, despite your location whether you are in the wilderness or not you shall drip with abundance. Even if you find yourself in the valley, you shall drip with abundance. In your wealthy place, pasture, you shall drip with abundance. So regardless of your location or circumstance, you shall drip with abundance. My year, your year has been crowned with God's goodness, and my paths, and your paths shall drip with abundance.

Therefore, I speak to the blessings which are mine and command them to come forth now! That my abundant harvest, anointing, divine health, healing, victory, prosperity, success and favor have to come now! I speak blessings, increase and grace to my savings accounts, wallets and pockets. I speak millionaire status to come forth now. I thank you Lord that you shall watch over your word to perform it, and it shall not return to you void. *Isaiah 55:10-11 (NKJV) ¹⁰ For as the rain comes down, and the snow from heaven, and do not return there, but water the earth, And make it bring forth and bud, That it may give seed to the sower and bread to the eater, ¹¹ So shall My word be that goes forth from My mouth; It shall not return to Me void, But it shall accomplish what I please, and it shall prosper in the thing for which I sent it.*

The Word of God shall prosper in you! You are qualified, entitled and worthy of the promises of God, of God's goodness and abundant blessings. Refuse to be beaten or cheated out of your inheritance. You have the right to claim God's benefits, you are worth it! You are important enough! You deserve it!

Jeremiah 5:24 (NKJV) He gives rain, both the former and the latter, in its season. He reserves for us the appointed weeks of the harvest. So as he gives the rain in its season you must understand and know that while you wait on the harvest which has been reserved for an appointed time, you shall drip in abundance. No matter what season you find yourself in, you shall drip in the abundance of God's goodness. *The Lord is good; for his mercy endures forever. Psalm 145:9 (NLT) The Lord is good to everyone. He shows compassion on all creation."* You need to expect His goodness to follow you this year and all the days of your life. ***Psalm 23:6 (NKJV) Surely goodness and mercy shall follow me all the days of my life: and I will dwell in the house of the Lord forever.*** Not only has he covered your year with His goodness but He also said, "Goodness and mercy shall follow you all the days of your life." It's because of God's goodness that the:

- Blind can see
- Lame can walk
- Deaf can hear
- Captives are free
- Storms cease
- Minds are free
- Marriages are restored
- Family relationships are restored and
- Children are healed, whole and healthy

Psalm 31:19 (NIV) How abundant are the good things that you have stored up for those who fear you that you bestow in the sight of all, on those who take refuge in you.

God has a specific plan for your life. Your pathway to the good life is included in that plan. In the name of Jesus, I declare that your mind is renewed by God's Word, and that you know His perfect will for your life. His purpose for you includes total life prosperity. Allow the Holy Spirit to lead you to the good life. His expected end for you does not include evil; instead, it is filled with peace. Receive God's anointing on your life. Receive the manifestation of this confession now, in Jesus name. Amen.

Ezekiel 12:28 (NKJV) This is what the Sovereign Lord says: None of my words will be delayed any longer; whatever I say will be fulfilled, declares the Sovereign Lord. That which He has spoken shall be performed (fulfilled) in your life in Jesus' name. Amen.

REFLECT AND JOURNAL:

Iris Dupree -Wilkes

Chapter 11

FROM CAPTIVE TO CAPTAIN
"You can't afford to go back"

No matter what happens in life you must always remember, you can't afford to go back. Going back symbolizes death. If the Lord has allowed you to be on top, why settle for things beneath? Why would you trade your mountain experience for the valley? My friend, don't allow anyone or anything to cause you to go back to lower your standards and to settle for less. God has better for you and you shall not go back!

After the crossing of the Red sea miracle, the children of Israel were in the wilderness whining and complaining about why they were in this place? They said, "We should have stayed in Egypt." Due to their blinded minds they could not fully understand or perceive that which the Lord had done for them. So when you can't perceive or fully understand what the Lord is doing in your life do you whine or complain like the wilderness wanderers? How do you respond? Do you retreat and begin to go backward, reminiscing about what once was, even though it was not the greatest or most healthy circumstances? Even if you don't understand the hand of God in your life, refuse to go backward. Going back spells corrupt living all over again. Understand that when you have been cleansed from corruption- evil living- you can't afford to go back to it. You must lift up a standard and move ahead.

In the life of Daniel, he refused to change his habit despite the king's decree. In other words he refused to go in a backward direction in an attempt to satisfy and please man. Therefore, the people rose up against Daniel in an attempt to take his very life. They did not just want to destroy his character, but this attack against Daniel was to take his life all together. But how many of you know that regardless of the plots of man (Satan) their wicked schemes will not win.

> *Daniel 6:3-9 (NKJV) ³ Daniel distinguished himself above the governors and satraps, because an excellent spirit was in him; and the king gave thought to setting him over the whole realm. ⁴ So the governors and satraps sought to find some charge against Daniel concerning the kingdom; but they could find no charge or fault, because he was faithful; nor was there any error or fault found in him. ⁵ Then these men said, "We shall not find any charge against this Daniel unless we find it against him concerning the law of his God." ⁶ So these governors and satraps thronged (gathered) before the king, and said thus to him: "King Darius, live forever! ⁷All the governors of the kingdom, theadministrators and satraps, the counselors and advisors, have consulted together to establish a royal statue and to make a firm decree, that whoever petitions any god or man for thirty days, except you, O king, shall be cast into the den of lions. ⁸ Now O king establish the decree and sign the writing so that it cannot be changed..." ⁹ Therefore King Darius signed the written decree.*

We see how they rose up against Daniel not because of his wrong actions but because:

- He distinguished himself above them, there was something different about him, he was set apart, there was a distinctive characteristic that was seen in him.This is not something Daniel made up, this was who he was.
- He had an excellent spirit in him, he was preeminent, and he possessed an oustanding quality where he was remarkably good, extraordinary.

Therefore because of these noted qualities in him, the "KING" gave thought of setting Daniel over the whole realm even governors and satraps who had been there for the king in times past. He preferred Daniel over them because of God's spirit in him. Daniel's experience, wisdom, knowledge, and leadership skills were greater than the norm. God ordained for Daniel to be in charge despite his circumstances. God had a plan and purpose for Daniel no matter what man plotted to do to him. God had the plan, and it was going to succeed in Daniel's life. So when the governors and satraps (enemy) heard this, they sought to find some charge against Daniel. Their motives were to stop him from being in charge, to stop his promotion which God had granted. Do you see the hand of the devil here? The royal statue stated that whoever petitions any god or man for thirty days except the king, will be cast into the den of lions. They gave Daniel thirty days of no communicating with his God. I'm sure Daniel felt like, are you kidding me, do you know what kind of havoc the devil can cause if I fail to seek my God for thirty days straight? Daniel refused to compromise about seeking his God. The enemy therefore, will do all he can to bring charges and accusations against you in an attempt to stop you from growing, from moving ahead, from prospering, from obtaining your God ordained promotion. Daniel was walking and functioning in his royal status as a king and priest to his God and those who did not know their status sought to take him down. Did Daniel go backward due to opposition? Did Daniel allow them to change his excellent spirit? What did Daniel do? How did Daniel fight the devil? You must learn how to fight the devil, he is real, and he wants nothing more than to destroy or kill you. So how do you fight? Let's see what Daniel did. First when he leaned of the decree he did not let it change his habit of seeking God.

Daniel 6:10-17 (NKJV) [10] Now when Daniel knew that the writing was signed, he went home. And in his upper room, with his windows open toward Jerusalem, he knelt down on his knees three times that day, and prayed and gave thanks Before his God, as was his custom since early days. [11] Then these men assembled and found Daniel praying and making supplication before his God. [12] And they went before the king, and spoke concerning the king's decree: "Have you not signed a decree that every man who petitions any god or man within thirty days except you, o king, shall be cast into the den of lions?" The king answered and said, "The thing is true, according to the law of the Medes and Persians, which does not alter." [13] So they answered and said before the king, "That Daniel, who is one to the captives from Judah, does not show due regard for you, O king, or for the decree that you have signed, but makes his petition three times a day." [14] And the king, when he heard these words, was greatly displeased with himself, and set his heart on Daniel to deliver him; and he labored till the going down of the sun to deliver him. [15] Then these men approached the king, and said to the king, "Know O king, that it is the law of the Medes and Persians that no decree or statue which the king establishes may be changed." [16] So the king gave the command, and they brought Daniel and cast him into the den of lions. But the king spoke, saying to Daniel, "Your God, whom you serve continually, He will deliver you." [17] Then a stone was brought and laid on the mouth of the den, and the king sealed it with the signets of his lords, that the purpose concerning Daniel might be changed.

Even though it may have been easier for Daniel to agree with the people and just simply obey the decree, he refused to compromise. Instead, he went home, and in his upper room, with his windows open toward Jerusalem, he knelt down on his knees three times that day. He prayed and gave thanks before his God, as was his custom since early days. Daniel continued to do what he knew to do. He refused to hide his actions; he did it willingly with his window wide open. He was not afraid of opposition, despite whose hands it came from. Daniel sought his God for that was what he knew to do. What are you doing in times of opposition? Whom are you seeking? Do you find yourself lowering your standards; are you compromising with the world to fit in, to be a part? What are you doing?

Now as a result of Daniel praying and making supplication before his God, the people went before the king and reminded him of the decree that was issued and could not be altered. The king was in total agreement of the decree, and they then informed him at that time that Daniel, making sure not to get him confused with anyone else said, ***"That Daniel, who is one of the captives from Judah, still makes his petition three times a day."*** So in other words Daniel, one of the prisoners, from Judah refuses to be kept in restraints or dominated.

How can he come over here as a prisoner and be placed in an authority position? We must take action O king, because "that Daniel" does not show regard for you. I'm sure at this point they felt oh yeah, we got him now. This is it for him, besides who does he think he is coming over here as a captive, a prisoner and taking charge? How can this be? So as you see in the life of Daniel he came to this land as a captive, as a prisoner, one that was held in captivity to those who were ruling over him, but he did not allow them to keep him in restraints as far as his belief in his God. Daniel still sought his God three times per day. Even in his captive state God was elevating and promoting him. Stop allowing what people say or do to cause your actions to change, to give in to their wicked schemes and behaviors. Stand firm with what you know is right. Refuse to compromise or to go backwards due to people.

When the king heard these words he was greatly displeased. He was troubled and set his heart and mind to deliver Daniel. He spent the rest of the day looking for a way to get Daniel out of this predicament; he labored till the going down of the sun to deliver him. But found no way to rescue Daniel. Then the evil men approached the king again reminding him of the decree and how they must move on with it for it cannot be changed. The king had no choice but to move ahead, despite how he felt in his heart. He gave the command to cast Daniel in the den of lions. Den refers to an underground pit for wild animals with a hole at the top. But prior to throwing Daniel in, the king said to Daniel, ***"Your God, whom you serve continually, He will deliver you."*** While in the underground pit, lions den, this hurtful place, circumstances should have been bad, so they thought. But I want you to know throughout the night, the king was fasting and he could not sleep like he usually did. He wanted Daniel's God to deliver him.

> ***Daniel 6: 19-23 (NKJV)*** *[19] **Then the king arose very early in the morning and went in hast to the den of lions. [20] And when he came to the den, he cried out with a lamenting voice to Daniel. The king spoke, saying to Daniel, "Daniel, servant of the living God, has your God, whom you serve continually, been able to deliver you from the lions?" [21] Then Daniel said to the king, "O king, live forever! [22] My God sent his angel and shut the lions' mouths, so that they***

have not hurt me, because I was found innocent before Him, and also O king, I have done no wrong before you." ²³ Now the king was exceedingly glad for him, and commanded that they should take Daniel up out of the den. So Daniel was taken up out of the den, and no injury whatever was found on him, because he believed in his God.

King Darius arose very early in the morning to check on Daniel to see if in fact his God did deliver him, he called out to Daniel saying, *"Daniel, servant of the living God, has your God, whom you serve continually, been able to deliver you from the lions?" ²¹ Then Daniel said to the king, "O king, live forever!* Daniel's response to the king was not in an angry tone for allowing such a decree to be passed, and to cause him to be placed in the pit, but instead he responded with a voice of excitement! *"O king, live forever! ²² My God sent his angel and shut the lions' mouths, so that they have not hurt me, because I was found innocent before Him, and also O king, I have done no wrong before you."* Because Daniel refused to go backward towards the way of man, his God delivered him. God had already ordained for Daniel to be promoted and the evil plot of men did not stop what God had for him. The lions in the den could not touch Daniel. God sent his angel and shut their mouth. God fought on behalf of his son Daniel, because he was found innocent before Him, and he did no wrong before the king. Daniel did not get mad and sin against the king, he trusted in his God. So despite how the devil may show up in man, you cannot allow their actions to persuade you to sin. You must walk upright despite the accusations, the lies, and their evil plots. God did not remove Daniel from being thrown in the pit, lions den, but instead helped him while in the midst of the storm. The storm could not overpower him. The thing that the enemy thought would happen to Daniel did not because His God was with him. Daniel moved forward and His God saved him and the king was exceedingly glad and made them take Daniel up out of the den. He came out with his hands lifted, he came out unharmed by the lions, and he came out free, delivered and whole, because He believed in his God! He was going to move from his position of captive to captain despite man's best attempt to stop it.

But look what happened to those men who caused this thing to happen to Daniel. ***Daniel 6:24 (NKJV) And the king gave the command, and they brought those men who had accused Daniel, and they cast them into the den of lions - them, their children, and their wives; and the lions overpowered them, and broke all their bones in pieces before they ever came to the bottom of the den.*** The very ones, who rose up against Daniel, had now spoken their own punishment. The king gave them the same opportunity as Daniel by now throwing them in the same lion's den, the pit. Not only were they going to be thrown in but their children and their wives as well. Their actions brought about harm to their entire family. After being thrown in the lion's den the lions overpowered them, and broke all their bones in pieces before they ever came to the bottom of the den. That's why you have to be careful of the seeds you sow, because what you make happen in the life of others it could very well be your downfall. Those who accused Daniel unjustly brought about their own ruin. The only weapon that Daniel used in this battle was that of prayer, trusting, and believing in his God.

You see people can take things, titles, homes, cars, etc. from you but they can't take what God has given you. The seed He has placed on the inside of His people. They could not destroy Daniel's excellent spirit. They could not take his knowledge, his wisdom or his leadership skills, no matter what they sought to do. Instead they allowed Daniel to make a lasting impact on the king so much so that he expressed himself to all the people: ***Daniel 6:25-28 (NKJV) 25 Then King Darius wrote: To all the peoples, nations, and languages that dwell in all the earth: peace be multiplied to you. 26 I make a decree that in every dominion of my kingdom men must tremble and fear before the God of Daniel. For He is the living God, and steadfast forever; His kingdom is the one which shall not be destroyed, and His dominion shall endure to the end. 27 He delivers and rescues, and He works signs and wonders in heaven and on earth, who has delivered Daniel from the power of the lions. 28 So this Daniel prospered in the reign of Darius in the reign of Cyrus the Persian.***

Daniel yet walked in his promotion, he was elevated, and he prospered greatly under Darius and Cyrus' rule. Daniel moved from being a captive to being the captain in charge. God had his hands on Daniel and those who opposed him could not bring any damage to him. You need to know on today, it's your time to move from captive to captain. You may have been held in captivity for a time, but on today God wants you to know its time to walk in your promotion, its time to be all that God said that you are.

- You are no longer a prisoner in your own mind, your mind is free, healed and delivered!
- You are no longer a prisoner to distractions, but you are rising above every distraction with strength and power!
- You are no longer a prisoner in your home, you have been released and the restraints have been removed!
- You are no longer a prisoner in your family; the light of Christ in you shall shine upon them!
- You are no longer a prisoner due to your past relationships, God has broken every chain, every spirit that has attached itself to you, woman of God, man of God, child of God be free!
- You are no longer a prisoner on your job, for I am opening doors and bringing promotions!
- You are no longer a prisoner in your ministry, for I have gifted you to rule and to reign!
- You my child are no longer a prisoner, but you are now free to move from captive to captain! The royalty of God has now been unveiled unto you. Walk in your royal anointing and do what God has ordained for you to do, in Jesus' name. Amen!

REFLECT AND JOURNAL:

Chapter 12

STATEMENTS OF ROYALTY
A Knowing of Who You Are

The less you know about your position in Christ the easier it is for Satan to keep you from the promises of God. God expects disciples of Jesus Christ to appropriate their new covenant rights by faith. Knowing your identity in Christ will help to eliminate wasted time, battles and undue struggles. It's time to get a knowing in your spirit about who you are. Quit believing the lies of the devil and start believing what God's Word says about you.

Ephesians 1:17-18 (NIV) [17] Father, may give you the Spirit of wisdom and revelation, so that you may know him better. [18] I pray that the eyes of your heart may be enlightened in order that you may know the hope to which he has called you, the riches of his glorious inheritance in his holy people.

In an attempt to know God better and to gain a proper understanding of who you are my prayer is that the Father will give you the spirit of wisdom and revelation. I pray that He will give you a capacity for vision beyond the natural eyesight, to see all that Christ has for you. The more you agree with God about your identity in Christ, the more your behavior will reflect your God-given identity.

When you understand who you are, it will affect the way you respond to problems, people and promises from God's Word. *Romans 12:2 "Be transformed by the renewing of your mind."* As the transformation process begins to unfold in your life, your response will be different, because you will have a greater understanding of who you are and who you belong to.

Do not be fooled nor look to man for your identity. You must begin speaking who you are in Christ Jesus. Say the same things that God says in His word. Declare it every day over your life. ***Proverbs 18:21(NKJV) Death and life are in the power of the tongue, and those who love it will eat its fruit.*** Is there death or life coming from your words?

Regardless of what you heard others say about you, you cannot continue to accept their lies. That is not who you are. Stop accepting death words spoken to you. Get a knowing of who you are!

When you begin speaking God's Word in your life, you will begin to act on the spoken word. As you hear yourself speaking the word over your life, your family and friends, it will get in your heart and as a result, will build your faith, change your thinking and your circumstances.

Ephesians 4:31-32,(NLT) *[31] **Get rid of all bitterness, rage, anger, harsh words, and slander, as well as all types of evil behavior. Instead (Insert your name) be kind to each other, tenderhearted, forgiving one another, just as God through Christ has forgiven you.***

On today, *(Insert your name_____)* boldly confesses that he/she will clean his/her spiritual temple. I declare I will get rid of all behavior, habits and attitudes that keep me in bondage. I declare that bitterness, rage, anger, harsh words and slander are no longer welcomed or accepted in my house. On today, I am cleaning my house. I lay aside the sin that tries to trap me. On today, I declare that I am loosed from the snares of wickedness, evil behaviors and empty thoughts of my past. I will no longer be entangled with the tricks, schemes or lies of the devil. On this day *(insert date_____)* I declare I will walk, talk, and act like the new creation that I am. ***I am a new creation because I am in Christ - 2 Corinthians 5:17. I am chosen by God, holy and dearly loved - 2 Corinthians 1:21. I have direct access to God - Ephesians 2:18. I have been redeemed and forgiven;*** therefore today *(insert date_____) (insert name*

_____) will renew his/her commitment to maintaining a clean house in Jesus name. Amen!

- The Lord GOD has given me the tongue of the learned, that I should know how to speak a word in season to *him who is* weary. He awakens me morning by morning, He awakens my ear to hear as the learned – Isaiah 50:4
- I am somebody - I am a spirit being alive to God
- I can do what God says I can do, He will perfect the work He has begun in me - Philippians 1:6
- I am a mighty child of God, I am blessed in the heavenly realms with every spiritual blessing - Ephesians 1:3
- I am a Royal Priesthood - 1 Peter 2:9
- I am a peculiar person - 1 Peter 2:9
- I am a holy nation - 1 Peter 2:9
- I am favored of the Lord
- I am accepted - Ephesians 1:6
- I am complete in Christ Jesus - Colossians 2:10
- I am redeemed and forgiven - Colossians 1:14
- I am a joint-heir with Christ - Romans 8:17
- I am more than a conqueror - Romans 8:37
- I am a doer of the word and blessed in my actions - James 1:22
- I am a spirit being, and I am growing - Colossians 2:7
- I am an overcomer - Revelations 12:11
- I am victorious - *1 John 5:4*
- I am not helpless - Philippians 4:13
- My mind and heart is protected with God's peace -Philippians 4:7
- I am an ambassador of Christ - 2 Corinthians 5:20
- I am always successful because I am seated in heavenly places with Christ Jesus
- I have been called out from darkness and placed into God's marvelous light, therefore I am living in the kingdom of God, and I shall reign on this earth as the king and priest that I am.
- I am living in peace
- I am filled with grace and mercy
- I am strong and do great exploits - Daniel 11:32
- I trust in the Lord with all my heart - Proverbs 3:5
- I do not lean to my own understanding - Proverbs 3:5

- In all my ways I acknowledge Him, and He directs my paths - Proverbs 3:6
- The Lord will perfect that which concerns me - Psalms 138:8
- I am far from oppression and fear cannot come near me or my family - Isaiah 54:14
- I am born of God and the evil one cannot touch me
- I have submitted to God and the devil flees from me because I resist him in the name of Jesus - James 4:7
- I am redeemed from the hand of the enemy - Psalms 107:2
- I am delivered from the powers of darkness - Colossians 1:13-14
- I am kept in safety wherever I go - Psalms 91:11
- I am daily overcoming the devil, for greater is He who is in me than he who is in the world 1 John 4:4
- I am a winner, for God always causes me to triumph in Jesus Christ - 2 Corinthians 2:14
- I will fear no evil for the Lord is with me, His word and His Holy Spirit comfort me - Psalms 23:4
- God's power works through me - Ephesians 3:7
- I decree and declare everything lost be restored sevenfold, every abused be judged, every disadvantage be reversed in Jesus name.
- I am healed by the stripes of Jesus, I walk in divine health - 1 Peter 2:24
- I am seeking God's kingdom first, and He adds good things to my life - Matthew 6:33
- I am anxious for nothing and pray about everything - Philippians 4:6
- I am a believer not a doubter - 2 Corinthians 4:13
- I am promised a full life - John 10:10, therefore, I will not allow my body to control my life
- I am taking the inheritance the Lord has given me, sickness, poverty, fear and worry has no power over me.
- I am prosperous spiritually, financially, and physically, because of my inheritance as a child of God.
- Lord, I confess your word over my finances; every attack will be turned into victory.
- In Jesus name, devil I command you to loose the wealth of this earth, and I command every hindering spirit, force to stop. In Jesus name, I bind you and render you ineffective against me.

- Wealth and riches shall be in MY house - Psalm 112:3
- I have no lack for God supplies all of my needs according to His riches in glory by Christ Jesus - Philippians 4:19
- I am the head and not the tail, I am above and not beneath -
- I am crowned with wealth - Proverbs 14:24
- He has given me the power to get wealth - Deutonomy 8:18
- Everything I do shall prosper - Psalms 1:3
- Let peace be within my walls and prosperity within my place - Psalms 122:7
- I am increasing, enlarging, becoming extremely successful and have entered into a state of prosperity - Psalms 92:12
- Financial wisdom from above flows to me
- I have finance favor from God today
- Divine appointments with wealth are set for me today
- I declare all my debts are paid in full
- I call myself debt free
- I have more than enough finances to do everything that God has called me to do
- I call my house and my property paid in full
- I receive raises, bonuses, inheritances, and checks in the mail
- I receive my increase, overflow, and more than enough in the area of my finances
- I resist lack and poverty for God supplies all my needs
- Satan I bind you from my finances, according to Matthew 18:18, and loose you from your assignment against me, in the name of Jesus. You will not keep any money from coming my way.

I press on toward the goal to win the prize to which God in Christ is calling us upward Philippians 3:14. I am pressing onward toward the goal, toward my healing, deliverance and freedom.

Continue to declare the right words over your life. When Jesus awoke on a boat in a stormy sea, He spoke to the wind and waves (Mark 4:39) and they heard him. Not only did the winds and waves hear His voice, but they immediately obeyed as well. The right words coming from your mouth will produce tremendous results. Do not use your mouth to say unauthorized, unholy or negative things about yourself or others. Confess daily and obey God's word, as you do, your words will be empowered by the spirit to produce changes wherever you send them. Address situations that need a change by your words. Use your tongue to confess your way into your desired breakthrough. Talk to your body, your home, your business, and your health. Declare God's word over your life everyday. I declare you are making progress and moving forward, onward in Jesus name.

You will keep believing and saying what God has said in His word. You will believe regardless of situations, feelings, and the opinions of others. Jesus will bring the promise to pass over the words in which you have spoken because you have gained a knowing of who you are.

REFLECT AND JOURNAL:

ABOUT THE AUTHOR

IRIS DUPREE-WILKES is consumed with an overwhelming urgency to get the "good news" into the hands, hearts, and minds of every man, woman, boy and girl on the face of this earth. She was born the youngest of five children to Connie Mack and Olivia Dupree in Greenville, North Carolina. She is married to Michael Wilkes and they have two beautiful children O'Mar Damon and Alexis DaiZnae'.

She accepted the Lord as her own personal savior in 1996, under the leadership of her pastors Apostle Charles and Lisa Lewis (ACM). At this time a seed was planted on fertile ground and was nurtured over the years. However it was not until after her father passed in 1999 that the seed began to grow and she truly surrendered her all to God and began to put every thought and dream inspired by God to paper. Thus, Iris Dupree-Wilkes, the author was born.

She is committed to the work of the Lord and is always mindful of the great commission and is diligent in encouraging those surrounded by her to do the same. In 2003 she accepted the call from God to minister and delivered her initial sermon entitled "Get Up and Lets Go". She has been going strong ever since.

Minister Iris Wilkes currently serves as the Care Ministry Coordinator and serves as a teacher for the Education Department at Antioch Church Ministries. She gladly accepts any opportunity which will enable her to put a tract into the hands of those she encounters.